1004956114

SCIENCE
FOUNDATIONS

The Genetic Code

SCIENCE FOUNDATIONS

The Big Bang
Evolution
The Genetic Code
Germ Theory
Gravity
Heredity
Light and Sound
Natural Selection
Planetary Motion
Plate Tectonics
Radioactivity
Vaccines

SCIENCE
FOUNDATIONS

The Genetic Code

PHILL JONES

CHELSEA HOUSE
PUBLISHERS
An imprint of Infobase Publishing

Science Foundations: The Genetic Code

Copyright © 2011 by Infobase Publishing

Chelsea House
An imprint of Infobase Publishing
132 West 31st Street
New York, NY 10001

Library of Congress Cataloging-in-Publication Data
Jones, Phill, 1953–
   The genetic code / Phill Jones.
      p. cm. — (Science foundations)
   Includes bibliographical references and index.
   ISBN 978-1-60413-084-3 (hardcover)
   1. Genetic code—Popular works. I. Title. II. Series.
   QH450.2.J66 2010
   572.8'633—dc22   2010015734

Chelsea House books are available at special discounts when purchased in bulk quantities for businesses, associations, institutions, or sales promotions. Please call our Special Sales Department in New York at (212) 967-8800 or (800) 322-8755.

You can find Chelsea House on the World Wide Web at
http://www.chelseahouse.com

Text design by Kerry Casey
Cover design by Ben Peterson
Composition by EJB Publishing Services
Cover printed by Bang Printing, Brainerd, MN
Book printed and bound by Bang Printing, Brainerd, MN
Date printed: November 2010
Printed in the United States of America

10 9 8 7 6 5 4 3 2 1

This book is printed on acid-free paper.

All links and Web addresses were checked and verified to be correct at the time of publication. Because of the dynamic nature of the Web, some addresses and links may have changed since publication and may no longer be valid.

Contents

The Code of Cells

Y ou are about to read a story about a code. In communications, a code is a system for converting information from one form to another. Words and phrases may be replaced with numbers, symbols, or code words. In the United States, one of the most commonly used codes is the Zoning Improvement Plan Code, or ZIP Code. The first ZIP Codes of 1963 had five digits. The first digit stood for a large region of the country —the area from the Northeast (0) to the West coast (9). The second two digits signified certain densely populated areas within the large regions. The final two digits stood for post offices or postal zones.

Codes have different uses. ZIP Codes and common e-mail codes squeeze a lot of data into a brief form. Other codes convey secrets. During the American Revolution, spies sent messages to General George Washington using a dictionary code. In this system, a coded message appeared as numbers that indicated the locations of words in a dictionary. Only the message's sender and intended receiver knew which edition of a particular dictionary to use.

The **genetic code** is a very different type of code. The genetic code is a code for genes. A **gene** can be pictured as a piece of a **deoxyribonucleic acid** (DNA) molecule that contains coded instructions for synthesizing a **protein**. Proteins are molecules that carry out many functions that are required to sustain life. The genetic code is a product of evolution. On Earth, most living things use the same genetic code. The widespread use of the genetic code has

7

enabled humans to alter characteristics of many types of life forms. Genetically altered bacteria, plants, and even an entire animal like a goat, can be used to produce medicines. Honeybees have been designed to resist diseases. Modified yeast cells can detect bombs. An understanding of the genetic code has also enabled scientists to devise new ways for treating diseases.

A VOYAGE INTO AN ANIMAL CELL

The story of the genetic code begins with the cell. It is within a cell that DNA's genetic code is translated into a recipe for making proteins, which perform all of a cell's vital functions. The word *cell* has a humble beginning. One day, the seventeenth-century English scientist Robert Hooke decided to investigate cork. "I took a good clear piece of Cork, and with a Pen-knife sharpen'd as keen as a Razor, I cut a piece of it off," Hooke reported in his book *Micrographia* (1665). "I could exceeding plainly perceive it to be all perforated and porous, much like a Honey-comb." The pores reminded Hooke of the orderly group of cells that monks used for their living quarters. Thus, he decided to call the pores "cells."

Today, scientists know that cells are the building blocks of animal organs and tissues. One cell can function independently of other cells. However, cells can also interact with each other to perform a task. Muscle cells, for example, work together to produce movement. Groups of brain cells act as a team to interpret signals sent by nerve cells from the eyes, resulting in vision.

A membrane covers the outside of an animal cell. The membrane retains a cell's contents, including a jellylike mix of water and proteins called **cytosol**. If the membrane becomes damaged, cytosol oozes from the cell. The loss of cytosol disrupts the vital functions of the cell's components.

A cell is organized like a factory. A factory is divided into departments with different functions. One department may oversee the company's finances, another takes care of hiring, another department maintains a computer network, and another manufactures a product.

In a similar way, a cell is organized into compartments that perform different jobs required for the cell's survival. Factories have

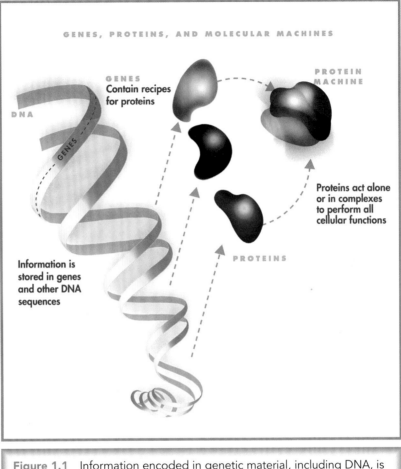

GENES, PROTEINS, AND MOLECULAR MACHINES

GENES
Contain recipes
for proteins

DNA

GENES

PROTEIN
MACHINE

Proteins act alone
or in complexes
to perform all
cellular functions

Information is
stored in genes
and other DNA
sequences

PROTEINS

Figure 1.1 Information encoded in genetic material, including DNA, is translated into proteins (in the form of amino acid sequences) by living cells through a set of rules called the genetic code.

walls and cubicles to separate different functions. Cells have membranes that divide tasks among small organ-like structures called **organelles**. A cell, like a factory, manufactures products. Protein is one of the products that are made by a cell. Five organelles play vital roles in the synthesis of proteins.

- **Mitochondria** are jelly bean-shaped organelles that process molecules obtained from food to supply energy to the cell. They power the process of protein production.

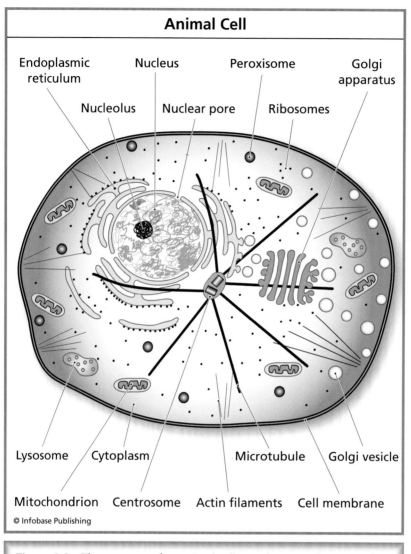

Animal Cell

Endoplasmic reticulum Nucleus Peroxisome Golgi apparatus

Nucleolus Nuclear pore Ribosomes

Lysosome Cytoplasm Microtubule Golgi vesicle

Mitochondrion Centrosome Actin filaments Cell membrane

© Infobase Publishing

Figure 1.2   The structure of an animal cell reveals a complex array of organelles suspended in cytosol and enclosed by the cell membrane.

- The **endoplasmic reticulum** is a collection of folded membranes. It is here that the cell synthesizes many proteins.
- **Golgi bodies** are disk-shaped structures that aid in the delivery of the cell's proteins. Certain proteins are modified

in Golgi bodies (or apparatus) to prepare the proteins for export outside the cell.

- **Lysosomes** digest old organelles, ingested food particles, and engulfed materials from the outside. These organelles break down complex chemicals to simple chemicals that the cell can use to make new products. A lysosome is part of the cell's recycling center.
- Last but not least is the **nucleus**. This organelle is the cell's command center. The nucleus stores genetic material that instructs the cell to make certain proteins.

Just as a cell has an outer cell membrane, a membrane called the **nuclear envelope** surrounds the nucleus. The nuclear envelope separates the nucleus from other parts of the cell. In fact, the inside of an animal cell can be considered to have two basic parts: a nucleus and **cytoplasm**. Cytoplasm is simply the cytosol and organelles found outside the nucleus.

The nucleus cannot be totally isolated from the cytoplasm. After all, the nucleus is the command center. Pores in the nuclear envelope allow certain molecules to slip outside the nucleus and into the cytoplasm. These molecules pass on instructions from the genetic material to the protein-making machinery.

The instructions of the genetic material are stored in DNA. Typically, the DNA in a nucleus can be found in **chromatin**, a mixture of DNA and proteins. Under the microscope, chromatin has a wiry, fuzzy appearance. When a cell is getting ready to reproduce itself by splitting into two cells, the chromatin compacts into the form of **chromosomes**. Most human cells typically have 46 chromosomes. It is the DNA in the chromosomes that determines the physical appearance and health of a person. The DNA of each cell contains the complete set of instructions for an individual's body.

Another important part of a cell is the **cytoskeleton** in the cytoplasm, which provides structure (like a skeleton) and movement (like muscles). The cytoskeleton is composed of long proteins. These protein cables form tracks that allow molecules and organelles to move within a cell. The proteins also help to form extensions of the cell membrane that enable certain cells to travel.

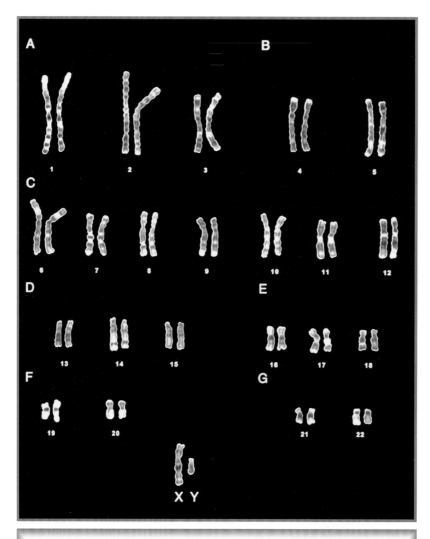

Figure 1.3 This image shows an enhanced magnification of human chromosomes. Most human cells contain 23 pairs of chromosomes. The mother and father contribute one chromosome to each pair.

CELL REPRODUCTION

Somatic Cells Split

The cytoskeleton performs another important role: It enables cells to have different shapes. Pipe-like protein structures form a scaffold that molds a cell to a shape suitable for the cell's function. Consider the muscles attached to bones in an arm or leg. The muscle contains hundreds or thousands of muscle fibers that are long,

Scientists Find Ancient, Frozen Bacteria

Bacteria are single-celled life forms that have a simple structure. Unlike an animal cell, a bacterial cell lacks a nucleus and other organelles with membranes. Bacteria store their genetic material in the form of a circle of DNA, rather than in the complex chromosomes that are found in animal cells. A bacterial cell basically consists of cytoplasm confined within an inner cell membrane and an outer, rigid cell wall. The cytoplasm contains DNA, proteins, and other molecules that are required for the bacteria to survive and to reproduce.

While simple in form, bacteria have lived on the Earth for a very long time. Scientists estimate that bacteria may have inhabited the planet for 3.5 billion years. An analysis of ancient bacteria could provide insights into evolution. The challenge is to find specimens.

A worldwide team of scientists searched for ancient life by drilling through ice in Siberia, Canada, and Antarctica. They collected samples of permafrost, which is soil that is permanently frozen at subzero temperatures. The scientists thought that permafrost offered the best chance for finding primeval bacteria, or at least ancient bacterial DNA. They were correct.

In 2007, the University of Copenhagen's Eske Willerslev announced that his team found active bacteria with intact DNA that was buried in permafrost samples. The specimens seem to be at least half a million years old, making them the oldest living organisms discovered to date. The discovery has implications about life beyond Earth. For example, Mars and the Jupiter moon Europa also have permafrost and ice. Therefore, could Mars and Europa harbor microbes, active but hidden at subzero temperatures?

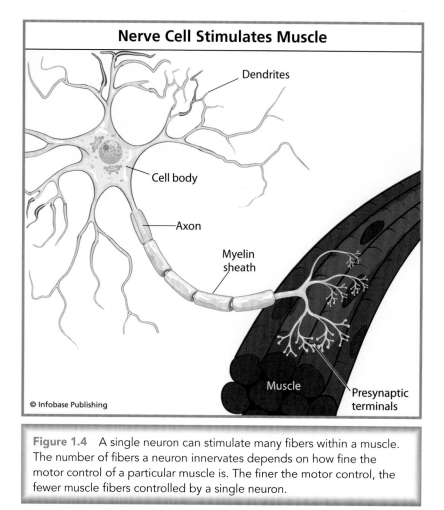

Nerve Cell Stimulates Muscle

Dendrites

Cell body

Axon

Myelin sheath

Muscle

Presynaptic terminals

© Infobase Publishing

Figure 1.4 A single neuron can stimulate many fibers within a muscle. The number of fibers a neuron innervates depends on how fine the motor control of a particular muscle is. The finer the motor control, the fewer muscle fibers controlled by a single neuron.

cylinder-shaped cells. A nerve cell has a very different shape; it looks a little like an elephant. Although most of the nerve cell is globular, the cell has a long, thin extension called an **axon**. The axon, which can extend to three feet (one meter), transfers an electrical signal from the cell body to a muscle fiber or to another nerve cell.

A muscle cell or a nerve cell is an example of a **somatic cell**. The majority of cells in an animal's body are somatic cells. (The exceptions are egg cells and sperm cells, which are also called **gametes**.) Somatic cells reproduce to support the development and maintenance of the body. Cells form gametes to ensure continuation of the species.

Cells reproduce themselves by the method of **mitosis**. In mitosis, a cell duplicates its DNA and divides into two cells, known as daughter cells. The nucleus of each daughter cell carries the same genetic information held by the nucleus of the original, parent cell.

Humans store their genetic information in the DNA of 24 different chromosomes:

- 22 chromosomes identified by number from largest to smallest,
- an X chromosome, and
- a Y chromosome.

Most human cells have a nucleus that contains 23 pairs of chromosomes, or 46 individual chromosomes. Egg cells and sperm cells have only 23 chromosomes each. At conception, an egg cell (which has chromosomes 1 to 22 and an X chromosome) and a sperm cell (which has chromosomes 1 to 22 and either an X chromosome or Y chromosome) fuse to form a cell that has the full set of 46 chromosomes—23 from each parent. A typical female has inherited one X chromosome from each parent, whereas a typical male has inherited an X chromosome from his mother and a Y chromosome from his father.

In mitosis, a cell prepares to divide by duplicating its DNA contents. Long molecules of DNA compress into densely packed chromosomes. The membrane that surrounds the nucleus—the nuclear envelope—breaks down. Like strands of a spider's web, cytoskeletal protein cables extend out from two sides of the cell and attach to chromosomes. The protein strands pull chromosomes to different sides of the cell, so that each side has a copy of the cell's DNA. The cell membrane tightens inward around the middle of the cell, pinching it into two spheres. When the cell membrane meets itself in the middle of the cell, it fuses and splits the old cell into two cells. The nuclear envelope reforms in each cell to hold its genetic information.

Formation of Gametes

Another type of cell division is called **meiosis**. Cells divide by meiosis to form egg cells and sperm cells. Meiosis proceeds in two stages to create four daughter cells. In humans, each of the four daughter

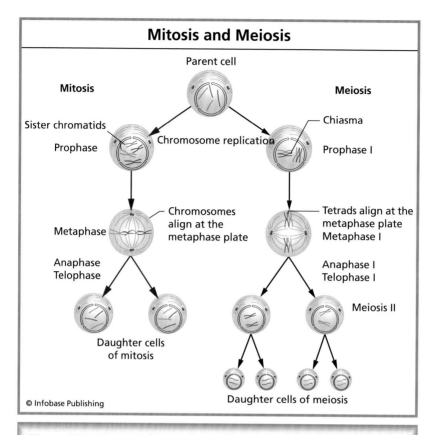

Figure 1.5   Mitosis (*left*) is a process that results in the formation of two new cells, each having the same number of chromosomes as the parent cells. Stages of mitosis include prophase, metaphase, anaphase, and telophase. Meiosis (*right*) consists of two divisions (meiosis I and meiosis II) and results in four daughter cells each containing the haploid number of chromosomes.

cells contains 23 chromosomes, or half the number of chromosomes found in typical somatic cells. If meiosis did not halve the number of chromosomes, then the number of chromosomes would double with each generation.

The first stage of meiosis is similar to mitosis. DNA duplicates to create twice the number of chromosomes, and the nuclear membrane breaks down. Web-like proteins attach to chromosomes and pull them to two sides of the cell. An important difference between mitosis and meiosis concerns the way that the web-like proteins divide chromosomes into the two sides of the cell. In mitosis, the two sets of chromosomes are identical. In the first stage of meiosis, the web-like proteins do not divide the chromosomes into two identical sets.

As an example, suppose that a somatic cell contains only one type of chromosome, called chromosome 1. The cell would have two copies of the chromosome—one from the mother and one from the father. Call them chromosome 1m and chromosome 1f, respectively. The cell gets ready to divide, and its DNA duplicates. Now, the cell contains two copies of chromosome 1m and two copies of chromosome 1f.

In mitosis, each side of the cell gets one copy of chromosome 1m and one copy of chromosome 1f. When the cell divides, the two daughter cells contain identical DNA. That is, each daughter cell has one copy of chromosome 1m and one copy of chromosome 1f.

Meiosis works differently. In the first stage of meiosis, each side of the cell gets two copies of chromosome 1m or two copies of chromosome 1f. When the cell divides, the daughter cells do not contain identical DNA.

What does this say about the first stage of meiosis in a human cell? Consider a female human cell. DNA duplicates to create the following chromosomes:

- two copies of chromosomes 1 to 22 inherited from the mother,
- two copies of chromosomes 1 to 22 inherited from the father,
- two copies of the X chromosome inherited from the mother, and
- two copies of the X chromosome inherited from the father.

After the first stage of meiosis, each daughter cell will have two copies of chromosomes 1 to 22 and two copies of an X chromosome. Each cell contains some chromosomes inherited from the mother and some chromosomes inherited from the father.

To complete the picture, consider a male human cell dividing in the first stage of meiosis. In this case, DNA duplicates to create the following chromosomes:

- two copies of chromosomes 1 to 22 inherited from the mother,
- two copies of chromosomes 1 to 22 inherited from the father,
- two copies of the X chromosome inherited from the mother, and
- two copies of the Y chromosome inherited from the father.

After the cell divides, each daughter cell will have two copies of chromosomes 1 to 22—some of them inherited from the father and

Mitochondrial DNA Assists CSIs

Mitochondria are unusual organelles. They have a size and shape similar to certain bacteria, and they have their own DNA, which is also similar in structure to bacterial DNA. Scientists propose that mitochondria might have originated from bacteria swallowed by primitive cells with nuclei. Instead of digesting the bacteria, these ancient cells formed a partnership that benefited the cells and the bacteria.

A typical human cell contains one nucleus and hundreds of identical mitochondria, each containing four or five copies of mitochondrial DNA (mtDNA). Scientists can analyze mtDNA isolated from biological samples that lack a sufficient amount of nuclear DNA for analysis. As a result, mtDNA analysis can be performed on shed hairs; bones and teeth subjected to high temperatures and other harsh conditions; and charred remains. Even fingerprints can yield mtDNA. Analysis of mtDNA has proved useful in investigations of new crimes and cold cases.

The technique does have a drawback. Suppose that investigators collect a biological sample from a crime scene. Nuclear DNA analysis can match the DNA of the sample with DNA from a suspect, since everybody's DNA is unique to them. Recent studies indicate that even identical twins can possess small differences in nuclear DNA.

some of them from the mother. One daughter cell will contain two copies of the X chromosome and the other will contain two copies of the Y chromosome.

The second stage of meiosis is simple. Each daughter cell divides its set of chromosomes equally between two cells, so that each cell contains the same DNA. Each of the four daughter cells contains half the number of chromosomes of the original cell. In males, the four cells will develop into sperm cells, while the cells develop into egg cells in females.

Unlike nuclear DNA, however, mtDNA is not unique. Typically, mtDNA is identical among maternally related people, such as a brother and a sister, or a mother and her child. This is because mtDNA is usually inherited only from the mother.

In the process of fertilization, a sperm's nuclear DNA enters the egg and combines with the egg's nuclear DNA. Most of the sperm's mitochondria are left outside the egg; the small numbers of sperm mitochondria that enter the egg are usually destroyed. So, the fertilized egg typically contains only maternal mtDNA.

Some of the cold cases aided by mtDNA analysis are so cold that they are part of history. One historical case concerned the death of the outlaw Jesse James. According to one tradition, Robert Ford, a member of the James brothers' gang, shot Jesse James in the back of the head on April 3, 1882. The body was transported to Kearney, Missouri, James's birthplace, and buried in the front yard of the family farm. Some people, however, claimed that Ford had actually shot the wrong man.

To explore such claims, researchers obtained two teeth and two hairs recovered from the James farm grave. They isolated mtDNA from the samples and then compared the mtDNA with mtDNA donated by living maternal relatives of Jesse James. The results suggest that the teeth and hair had indeed belonged to the outlaw.

CELL DIVISION AND INFORMATION TRANSFER

The complex process of meiosis ensures that genetic information passes from one generation to the next. Mitosis ensures that genetic information passes from a somatic cell to its two daughter cells. Today, scientists take these concepts for granted. Yet, it required a century of scientific research from the discovery of the existence of genes to an understanding of how a cell uses data stored in a gene to synthesize a protein to discover these concepts. And it all started with a monk who bred garden peas.

Discovering the Links between Inheritance, DNA, and Protein

THE NATURE OF INHERITANCE

A Monk Discovers the Basic Laws of Heredity

Since the beginning of agriculture, farmers have known that animals and plants can be bred to produce desirable traits. The subject of heredity has also attracted experts in science for thousands of years. By the 1700s, scientists knew that the combination of gametes—egg cells and sperm cells—produced a new life form. But a vital question remained unanswered: How did the parents' characteristics transfer to offspring? According to one school of thought, sperm cells contained all hereditary contributions for a new generation. Others argued that egg cells held all the required ingredients for heredity. A stocky monk named Gregor Mendel showed that neither group had it right.

Gregor Mendel was born in 1822 in a village near the border between northern Moravia and Silesia. (Today, this part of Europe is the Czech Republic.) After he completed high school, Mendel entered an Augustinian monastery that was dedicated to researching and teaching science. Mendel also studied science at the University of Vienna. He tried to earn teaching credentials, but he failed his exams.

After he returned to the monastery, Mendel decided to research the nature of heredity. In 1856, he turned a garden into his laboratory and bred pea plants. Mendel chose the common garden pea because the plant has a variety of easily identifiable traits or characteristics, including flower color, pea pod shape, seed color, and plant height. He could readily buy peas in a range of colors and shapes. Another benefit of the pea plant is that it produces both sperm and eggs. This gave Mendel the choice of self-crossing a plant—uniting egg cells and sperm cells from one plant—or crossing two plants by mixing their gametes, a term Mendel coined to describe egg and sperm cells.

For his experiments, Mendel selected traits that appeared as one of two forms, but not as a mixture of the two. The traits included purple flowers or white flowers, tall stems or short stems, yellow seeds or green seeds, and others. In his early studies, Mendel examined the inheritance of two types of seed shapes: smooth and wrinkled. He crossed plants that only produced smooth seeds with plants that always made wrinkled seeds. This breeding experiment resulted in "first generation" plants that only made smooth seeds. He planted the seeds and allowed the plants to grow. Then, he crossed this first generation with itself, a self-cross. The experiment yielded 5,474 smooth seeds and 1,850 wrinkled seeds. That is, he found a 3:1 ratio of smooth and wrinkled seeds.

In another series of experiments, Mendel crossed tall plants with short plants. The offspring were all tall. Then, he grew a second generation from self-crossed offspring. This generation had tall and short plants in a ratio of about 3:1.

It became clear that certain seed shape and plant height traits skipped the first generation. To explain his results, Mendel created two terms to describe types of traits: **dominant** and **recessive**. The production of smooth seeds is an example of a dominant trait. The cross between plants that produce smooth seeds and plants that produced wrinkled seeds resulted in plants that only produced smooth seeds. In the experiment, the production of wrinkled seeds is the recessive trait; it disappeared in the first generation and reappeared in the second generation.

Over eight years, Mendel grew 28,000 plants, tested 34 varieties of peas, and studied 7 characteristics. From these experiments, he made the following observations:

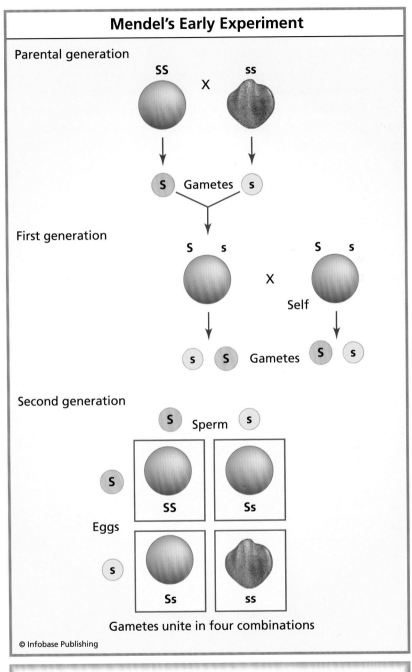

Mendel's Early Experiment

Parental generation

SS   X   ss

S   Gametes   s

First generation

S   s   S   s

X

Self

s   S   Gametes   S   s

Second generation

S   Sperm   s

S

| | SS | Ss |

Eggs

s

| | Ss | ss |

Gametes unite in four combinations

© Infobase Publishing

Figure 2.1   Gregor Mendel's experiments with plants helped him understand more about dominant and recessive traits, including how they are passed on over generations.

- The first generation exhibited one of the two traits of a parent plant, the dominant trait.
- When a parent plant had a recessive trait, the trait skipped a generation and reappeared in the offspring of a self-crossed first generation in about 25% of the plants (the 3:1 ratio).
- Experiments produced the same results regardless of which parent donated female gametes and which parent donated male gametes.

Mendel concluded that separate factors, or "units of inheritance," controlled the appearance of traits. The factors were inherited in pairs—one factor from the male parent and one factor from the female parent. Members of a pair of factors separate from each other during the formation of gametes. The combination of an egg cell and sperm cell produces a cell with a pair of the factors. Today, these factors are known as genes.

Consider one of Mendel's experiments with purple flowers and white flowers in the light of current knowledge. Mendel bred a parent line of pea plants that could only produce plants with purple flowers. These plants had two copies of the gene responsible for purple flowers. After meiosis, each gamete contained one copy of the "purple flower gene" (P). Mendel also bred a parent line of pea plants that only produced plants with white flowers. The plants had two copies of the white flower gene (W) and made gametes with one copy of the white flower gene. When the two lines were bred together, their offspring had one copy of the P gene and one copy of the W gene. Yet, they produced only purple flowers, because the purple flower trait is a dominant trait. The gametes produced by this first generation then contained either a P gene or a W gene. Mendel's self-cross of the first generation produced four possible combinations of P genes and W genes:

- P gene + P gene (PP)
- P gene + W gene (PW)
- W gene + P gene (WP)
- W gene + W gene (WW)

Since the purple flower trait is dominant over the white flower trait, 75% of the second generation had purple flowers (PP, PW, and WP), and 25% had white flowers (WW).

Mendel had discovered the rule that heritable traits are independently inherited. He also found mathematical rules that govern inheritance. Yet, he did not receive recognition for his success during his life. In fact, Mendel's work went largely ignored for more than 30 years. Other scientists had to catch up with the monk.

Locating Genes on Chromosomes

Mendel proposed that parents passed certain factors to their offspring and that these factors caused the appearance of traits. Gametes must contain these factors. But where are the factors located in the cell?

During the late nineteenth century, German scientist Theodor Boveri studied the growth of sea urchin eggs. He concluded that the nuclei of sperm cells and egg cells had the same amount of hereditary information. Egg cells and sperm cells have half the number of chromosomes, compared with other cells in the sea urchin. After scientists rediscovered Mendel's work in 1900, Boveri realized that

Left-Hand Gene

About 90% of people are right-handed, a little less than 10% prefer their left hand, and the remainder can use both hands with equal skill. Studies have shown that handedness is linked to a part of human chromosome 2. More than 40 scientists in 20 research organizations around the globe investigated chromosome 2 for clues about handedness. In 2007, they announced the discovery of a gene called LRRTM1. Research team leaders suggested that the gene affects the development of the human brain in a way that increases the chances that a person will be left-handed.

The human brain does not operate by distributing functions uniformly; the brain is asymmetrical. In right-handed people, the left side of the brain controls speech and language, whereas the right side regulates emotion. The pattern is often reversed in people who are left-handed. Scientists propose that LRRTM1 modifies the development of asymmetry in the human brain. In this way, the gene influences a preference for the use of the left hand or right hand.

Mendel's factors shared similarities with chromosomes: Gametes had half the amount found in somatic cells.

Meanwhile, Walter Sutton, a long-time Kansas resident, studied grasshopper cells at Columbia University in New York. In 1902, Sutton published a paper that showed how meiosis reduced chromosome number in gametes. He proposed that this reduction was related to Mendel's laws of inheritance, and that genes, the basis of heredity, reside in chromosomes.

Thomas Hunt Morgan confirmed that chromosomes contain genes. Morgan was born in Kentucky in 1866. He was the great grandson of Francis Scott Key, who had written the words to the American national anthem, "The Star-Spangled Banner." But it was science that interested Morgan. He trained as a biologist, and, in 1904, he accepted the position of professor of experimental zoology at Columbia University. A colleague convinced Morgan that if he wanted to understand the development of an animal, then he must study heredity.

Morgan decided that he would examine heredity in the fruit fly, an insect that eats decaying fruit. The flies are so small, about 0.12 inches (3 millimeters) long, that one thousand of them can be raised in a one-quart glass milk bottle. Another advantage of the fruit fly is that its somatic cells have only four pairs of chromosomes. Morgan wanted to study the relationship between mutations and changes in the chromosomes. A **mutation** is an alteration in a gene that can result in an altered protein.

After years of studying the tiny flies, Morgan discovered one that had white eyes, instead of the typical red eyes. He bred the white-eyed mutant with a red-eyed fly. The offspring had red eyes, suggesting that red eye color is a trait dominant to white eye color. Morgan then bred the first generation with itself. The second generation had red-eyed flies and white-eyed flies in a 3:1 ratio. Upon closer examination, he discovered that the white-eyed flies were all males. The white eye trait is linked to gender. Further experiments showed that yellow body color and a mutated wing structure are also linked to gender.

Morgan's studies revealed that genes reside in particular chromosomes. For instance, the gene that causes red eye color resides in the chromosome that determines the gender of a fly. He proposed

Dog Varieties Breed Questions About Genetics

One of the branches of the canine family tree includes coyotes, jackals, the gray wolf, and dogs. Scientists consider the dog to be the most recently evolved species of canines. Dogs may have appeared as recently as 40,000 years ago. Thanks to selective breeding by humans, modern dogs have a wide range of body shapes, coat colors, sizes, head shapes, leg lengths, and other traits. The number of variations seen in dogs may exceed that of all living land mammals. Humans began to breed dogs at least 15,000 years ago. Yet, most of today's common breeds probably first appeared only during the last 200 to 300 years.

Scientists are beginning to find genetic explanations for the many types of dogs. Consider the whippet, a breed developed during the late 1800s for racing. The whippet is a medium-sized dog with a slim build, a long neck, and a small head. The related bully whippet has a broad chest and highly developed leg and neck muscles. A key genetic difference between the two animals is that the bully whippet has a mutation in the gene for myostatin. Myostatin is a growth factor that limits an increase in muscle tissue. The whippet produces normal myostatin; the hulking bully whippet produces a mutated myostatin.

In another study, a research team tackled the genetic basis for variations in dog size. They analyzed DNA from over 3,000 dogs and 143 breeds. The dogs varied in size from the toy fox terrier, which has a height no greater than 11.5 inches (29.2 centimeters), to the male Irish Wolfhound, a dog that must have a height of at least 32 inches (81.3 cm) to qualify for the breed. Genetic analyses revealed another genetic mutation. This time, scientists found the mutation in the gene encoding a protein hormone, insulin-like growth factor-1. Other studies have shown that the hormone influences body size in mice and humans.

that chromosomes contained an assembly of genes arranged in a linear fashion. Certain genes could be found at certain places in certain chromosomes, just as particular homes can be found along a street. Further experiments showed that a chromosome—like a street—can be mapped. These studies paved the way for the huge effort to map all human genes to their chromosomes.

WHAT ARE GENES MADE OF?

In 1869, Swiss physician Johann Friedrich Miescher studied proteins in human white blood cells. While attempting to analyze the many types of proteins, he discovered a new substance. It appeared to originate from cell nuclei, so he called it **nuclein.** Other scientists discovered that the major part of nuclein is deoxyribonucleic acid (DNA). In 1923, a new staining procedure revealed that nuclear DNA is localized in chromosomes. This discovery by itself, however, did not prove that DNA had something to do with genes. After all, chromosomes contained large amounts of protein.

In 1928, an English medical officer named Frederick Griffith performed an experiment that revealed a property of genetic material in bacteria. While studying the bacteria that caused pneumonia, Griffith observed that the bacteria appeared in two forms. One form (R strain) had a rough surface and did not produce the disease, whereas a highly infective S strain had a capsule that coated its exterior and gave the bacteria a smooth appearance. The capsule was required for infection.

Griffith killed deadly S strain bacteria by boiling them. He injected the heat-killed bacteria cells into mice. The mice survived. Then, he injected mice with a mixture of living R strain bacteria cells and heat-killed S strain cells. This time, the mice died. From the bodies of the dead mice, Griffith recovered living R strain cells and living S strain cells. The living R strain cells had acquired genetic material from the killed S strain cells. The genetic material converted harmless R strain cells into deadly S strain cells. He called the transfer of genetic material **transformation**.

Oswald Avery, Maclyn McCarthy, and Colin MacLeod analyzed the transformation process in a laboratory at the Rockefeller Institute in New York during the 1940s. Bacterial extracts that

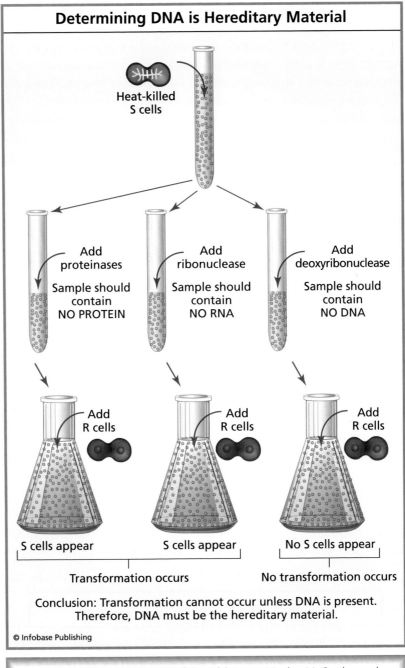

Determining DNA is Hereditary Material

Heat-killed
S cells

Add
proteinases

Sample should
contain
NO PROTEIN

Add
ribonuclease

Sample should
contain
NO RNA

Add
deoxyribonuclease

Sample should
contain
NO DNA

Add
R cells

Add
R cells

Add
R cells

S cells appear

S cells appear

No S cells appear

Transformation occurs

No transformation occurs

Conclusion: Transformation cannot occur unless DNA is present.
Therefore, DNA must be the hereditary material.

© Infobase Publishing

Figure 2.2   The experiments of Oswald Avery, Maclyn McCarthy, and Colin MacLeod indicated that DNA must be the hereditary material.

transformed bacteria contained protein, DNA, and **ribonucleic acid** (RNA). Therefore, protein, DNA, or RNA had the properties of genetic material. To eliminate suspects, the scientists used **enzymes**, proteins that increase the rates of chemical reactions. They treated extracts of S strain bacteria cells with one of three enzymes: a **protease** to digest protein, a **deoxyribonuclease** (DNase) to digest DNA, or a **ribonuclease** (RNase) to digest RNA. Then, they treated three groups of R strain cells with the extracts to see which retained the ability to transform the cells to S strain cells. Protease and RNase treatments had no effect. However, the DNase treatment deactivated the extract. DNA caused the transformation of bacterial cells.

The experiments with enzyme-treated extracts strongly suggested that DNA is the genetic material. Yet, many scientists resisted the idea. Any lingering doubts disappeared after American biologists Alfred Hershey and Martha Chase performed their experiments with bacteriophages. A **bacteriophage**, or "**phage**," is a type of virus that infects bacteria (*Bacteriophage* means "bacteria eater"). Like viruses that infect animal cells, a phage is composed of a **nucleic acid**—DNA or RNA molecules—surrounded by proteins. A phage is a parasite that attaches to bacteria and injects its genetic material. Once inside a bacterial cell, the phage's genetic material forces the bacteria's synthesis machinery to make more phages.

Did the phages inject nucleic acid, protein or both? To answer this question, Hershey and Chase used a type of phage composed of proteins and DNA. Protein and DNA differ chemically: proteins contain sulfur and very little phosphorus, whereas DNA lacks sulfur and contains a large amount of phosphorus. The scientists produced phages with radioactive sulfur in their protein coat and other phages with radioactive phosphorus in their DNA. They infected two **cultures** of bacteria with the two types of phages, and then poured the cultures into kitchen blenders. The blenders' blades created a violent whirlpool that broke off empty phage casings that clung to the bacteria's outsides. Hershey and Chase then used a centrifuge to separate phage bodies from the heavier bacterial cells. After centrifugation, they had pellets of bacteria and liquid with phages.

Next, the scientists looked at the distribution of radioactivity. In cultures infected by phages with radioactive sulfur, they found most of the radioactivity in the liquid. In cultures infected by phages with

Hershey-Chase Experiment

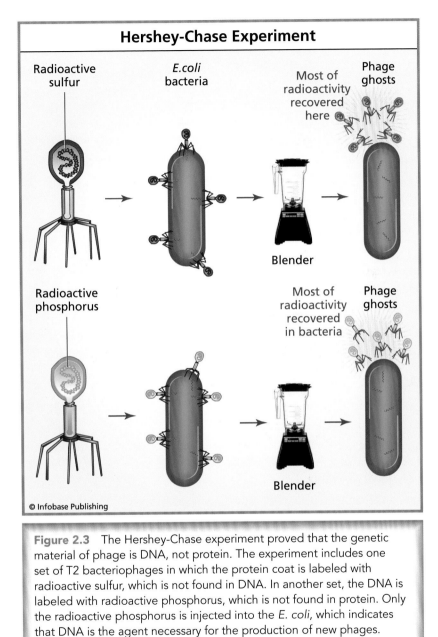

Radioactive sulfur

E.coli bacteria

Most of radioactivity recovered here

Phage ghosts

Blender

Radioactive phosphorus

Most of radioactivity recovered in bacteria

Phage ghosts

Blender

© Infobase Publishing

Figure 2.3 The Hershey-Chase experiment proved that the genetic material of phage is DNA, not protein. The experiment includes one set of T2 bacteriophages in which the protein coat is labeled with radioactive sulfur, which is not found in DNA. In another set, the DNA is labeled with radioactive phosphorus, which is not found in protein. Only the radioactive phosphorus is injected into the E. coli, which indicates that DNA is the agent necessary for the production of new phages.

radioactive phosphorus, they found most of the radioactivity in the bacterial pellet. Phage DNA entered bacteria, not the phages' proteins. DNA is the genetic material.

WHAT DOES DNA DO?

Almost 100 years passed between the time that Mendel began his garden pea studies and Hershey and Chase performed their phage experiment in 1952. During that time, scientists had learned about the genetic basis for inheritance. But how do genes exert control?

- "Units of inheritance"—genes—control the appearance of traits.
- Genes are inherited in pairs.
- Genes can be found in the chromosomes of cell nuclei.
- Genes are linked together on chromosomes.
- DNA of chromosomes—not chromosomal protein—carries genetic information.
- Genes made of DNA control the appearance of traits.

In 1909, British physician Archibald Garrod studied an inherited disorder in humans that causes urine to turn black when exposed to air. Garrod analyzed the urine of family members with and without the disorder. He proposed that the lack of an enzyme caused the condition, and that the loss of enzyme activity could be traced to a recessive gene. Normally, the enzyme degrades the chemical that gave urine the black color. Like Mendel's studies, Garrod's work was largely ignored for decades.

During the 1940s, American scientists George Beadle and Edward Tatum explored the connection between genes and enzymes. They selected a bread mold as their biological model to test the theory that genes and enzymes shared a one-to-one relationship. Beadle and Tatum treated mold spores with ultraviolet radiation or X-rays to induce mutations. They isolated mutant molds that could grow only if they were provided with vitamins or other supplements. Normal molds could make their own supplies of nutrients, suggesting that mutants had defects in the synthesis of nutrients. The scientists discovered that each mutant had an alteration in one gene. A mutation in one gene resulted in the loss of one type of active enzyme that normally produced chemicals vital for the mold's survival. Beadle and Tatum proposed that each gene directs the synthesis of a specific enzyme.

Other scientists later showed that genes controlled the synthesis of all proteins, not just enzymes. This insight raised an important question: How does a gene control the production of a protein? The answer lay in the genetic code.

Solving the Genetic Code Puzzle

AN EARLY IDEA ABOUT THE GENETIC CODE

The genetic code enables a cell to transform one type of information to another type of information. That is, the code provides the means for a cell to use the data stored in DNA to produce proteins. DNA and proteins are very different types of molecules. They differ in chemical components, structure, and function.

Yet DNA molecules and proteins do share a common feature: They are both polymers. A **polymer** is a large chemical that is made by combining smaller chemical units. In a way, a polymer is like a train. A train is formed by combining smaller cars. Similarly, a protein or a DNA molecule is formed by combining smaller chemicals. With a train, a mechanical device called a coupler connects the railway cars to each other. With protein and DNA, small chemicals link with each other by forming a **chemical bond**. These bonds are created when atoms of two chemicals share electrons. A protein forms when small molecules called **amino acids** connect with each other by chemical bonds.

A DNA molecule is a polymer composed of **nucleotides** linked by chemical bonds. Each nucleotide has three parts: (1) a **deoxyribose** sugar molecule, a 5-carbon sugar molecule called **ribose** that is missing a particular oxygen atom; (2) a phosphate molecule, a chemical

33

Deoxyribose Nucleotide

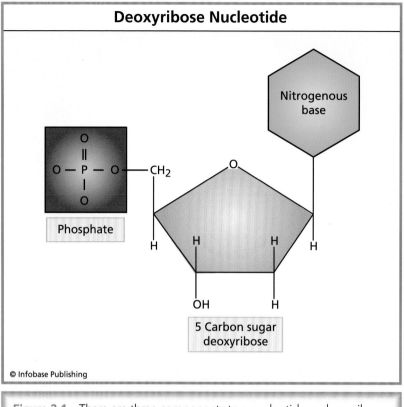

Nitrogenous base

Phosphate

5 Carbon sugar deoxyribose

© Infobase Publishing

Figure 3.1   There are three components to a nucleotide: a deoxyribose sugar molecule, a phosphate group, and a nucleotide base.

group that contains phosphorus; and (3) a molecule called a **base**, which contains nitrogen. The sugar group of one nucleotide binds with the phosphate group of another nucleotide. This means that a DNA molecule has a "sugar-phosphate-sugar-phosphate" structure. The structure is called the sugar-phosphate backbone of DNA.

The bases of nucleotides stick out from the sugar-phosphate backbone. A DNA molecule has four types of bases: adenine, cytosine, guanine, and thymine. Scientists refer to the bases by the first letter of their names. For example, "AGCTGA" indicates a small piece of DNA that has the base sequence "adenine-guanine-cytosine-thymine-guanine-adenine."

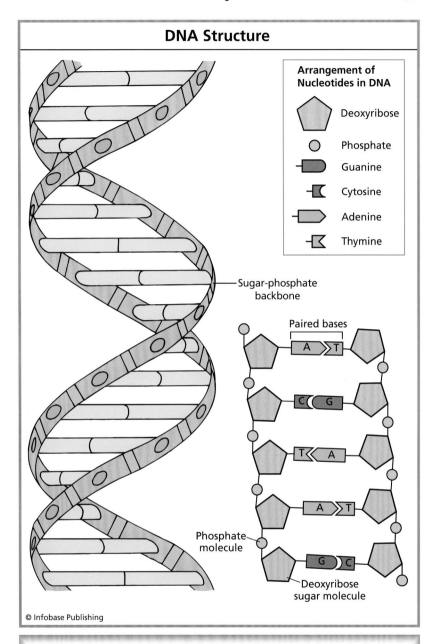

DNA Structure

Arrangement of Nucleotides in DNA

Deoxyribose

Phosphate

Guanine

Cytosine

Adenine

Thymine

Sugar-phosphate backbone

Paired bases

A T

C G

T A

A T

Phosphate molecule

G C

Deoxyribose sugar molecule

© Infobase Publishing

Figure 3.2 The structure of DNA resembles a ladder. The nucleotides twist in a double helix, joined together by base pairs of nucleotides. The "rungs" of the "ladder" are made up of these base pairs.

During the late 1940s, Erwin Chargaff, a scientist at Columbia University in New York City, analyzed DNA from many different sources. He studied the nucleotide contents of DNA from human, cow, salmon, yeast, and various bacteria. Chargaff found that DNA had several key features.

At that time, many scientists thought that DNA contained equal amounts of all four bases organized in a simple way. For example, a

Decoding a Biological Weapon

Burkholderia mallei is a type of bacteria that causes a disease known as glanders. This disease mainly affects horses, donkeys, and mules. The bacteria can inflict wounds in the lungs and may kill an animal by growing in its blood. Although *B. mallei* primarily infect animals, the bacteria can also infect humans and cause painful, fatal illness.

Historians suggest that *B. mallei* might have been an early biological weapon. During the American Civil War, a Union colonel wrote an interesting report saying that a retreating Confederate Army had left behind horses infected with glanders for the Union Army. During World War I, horses and mules that carried supplies might have been deliberately exposed to the disease. During World War II, the bacteria might have been used to infect horses, civilians, and prisoners of war.

The U.S. government classifies *B. mallei* as a possible biological weapon that may be used against people in the future. The infectious bacteria can travel in the air and enter a body through the skin, nose, and eyes. An infected person can be treated with antibiotics. To date, however, no treatment exists to prevent someone from getting the disease.

In 2004, scientists reported they had found the complete nucleotide sequence of *B. mallei* DNA. Studies of the DNA revealed details about sequences encoding the proteins that make the bacteria so deadly. The study of *B. mallei* DNA may allow scientists to devise more effective therapies for glanders.

DNA molecule might contain repeating blocks of AGCT. The DNA molecule would then have a form of AGCT AGCT AGCT [. . . .] If DNA did have such a simple structure, then it could not carry a code.

Chargaff's studies of DNA from various species revealed three clues about the nature of DNA. They are:

- DNA does not contain equal amounts adenine, cytosine, guanine, and thymine.
- DNA contains equal amounts of guanine bases and cytosine bases.
- DNA contains equal amounts of adenine bases and thymine bases.

Here are three examples of short DNA molecules that follow Chargaff's rules: (1) AGGTCCTATA, (2) GGGTCCCCGA, and (3) TTCCCAGAGG. Many combinations of bases can fulfill the rules.

After Chargaff proved that DNA is not such a simple molecule, scientists suggested that the bases in a DNA molecule could contain genetic information. One early idea about a genetic code was based on the fact that DNA molecules and proteins are polymers. Perhaps, the nucleotides of a DNA molecule provided a template—a type of mold—that attracted amino acids. Amino acids might bind with nucleotides like a piece of metal binds with a magnet. Strong chemical bonds could then form between amino acids to make a protein.

This early idea was interesting, but it was incorrect. Scientists needed more pieces of the puzzle before they could crack the genetic code.

THE DOUBLE HELIX OF DNA: ANOTHER PIECE OF THE PUZZLE

Exploring DNA's Secrets with X-rays

In May 1950, Swiss scientist Rudolph Singer attended a scientific meeting in London where he handed out samples of DNA that he had purified using a new technique. Maurice Wilkins, a scientist at King's College in London, took one of these samples and, working with a student named Raymond Gosling, began to study the DNA with the X-ray diffraction method.

Using X-ray diffraction to study DNA was an unusual approach. Typically at that time, scientists used X-ray diffraction to study the three-dimensional structure of crystallized proteins. Just as a beam of visible light scatters, or diffracts, after it hits a glass crystal, an X-ray beam breaks up after it hits a protein crystal. After the X-ray beam becomes scattered, it forms a diffraction pattern, which appears as a pattern of spots on an X-ray sensitive film. The details of the pattern give clues about the arrangement of atoms in the protein. Similarly, X-ray bombardment of DNA produced a diffraction pattern that gave clues about the organization of chemical components in the DNA molecule.

Gosling began to bombard purified DNA with X-rays to learn about the molecule's structure. He was soon joined by Rosalind Elsie Franklin, an expert in crystals. Franklin was born in London in 1920. During the 1940s, she studied the physical structure of coal at a British research organization. Later, she moved to Paris and developed an expertise in the use of X-rays to examine crystalline structures. After she arrived at King's College in January 1951, she started working with Gosling to analyze DNA. Their X-ray experiments produced an interesting result—DNA seemed to be shaped like a spiral or a helix.

Meanwhile, about 50 miles away, two scientists at Cambridge University had also developed an interest in DNA—the now-famous team of Francis Crick and James Watson. Francis Crick was born in Northampton, England, in 1916. He earned a bachelor's degree in physics and started work on his Ph.D. After World War II broke out, Crick worked on underwater mines for the British government. In 1949, he joined the Medical Research Council at England's Cambridge University. Once again, he began working for a Ph.D, this time with a focus on biology. It was at Cambridge that Crick met James Watson.

Born in Chicago, Illinois, James Watson began his life as a student at an early age: He was only 15 years old when he entered the University of Chicago in 1943. After graduating, he moved to Indiana University where he earned a Ph.D. while studying the effects of X-rays on bacteriophages.

On a visit to Italy in the spring of 1951, Watson met Maurice Wilkins and learned about the diffraction of X-rays by DNA. Watson joined the Medical Research Council in Cambridge, where he

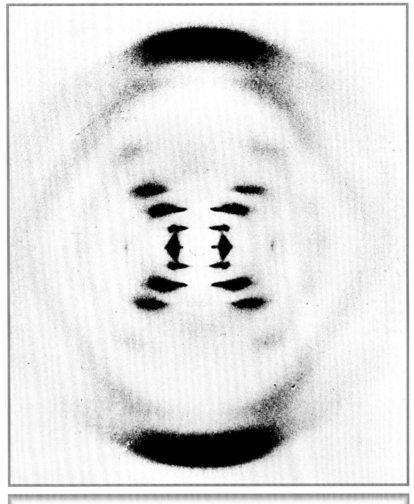

Figure 3.3   This X-ray diffraction image of DNA taken by Rosalind Franklin is called Photo 51. The image is famous because scientist Maurice Wilkins passed the image on to James Watson, who, along with Francis Crick, discovered the structure of a DNA molecule, based on information provided in the image.

was supposed to examine a protein using X-ray diffraction. Soon after Watson arrived, he and Crick became friends. They shared an interest in discovering the structure of DNA. After hearing Rosalind Franklin present the results of her X-ray studies of DNA, Watson and Crick built a model of DNA. Their DNA helix had three interwoven chains. At first, scientists ridiculed the model because it was not consistent with X-ray data and did not even obey basic rules of chemistry. Watson and Crick were ordered to stick to their assigned studies on proteins. However, they did not give up working on DNA.

The Double Helix of DNA Stores the Genetic Code

In February 1953, Crick received a copy of a King's College report that included Franklin's latest results. After reviewing the data, Crick decided that DNA might have two chains that ran in opposite directions.

Before thinking about the direction of a DNA chain, consider how a line of people can have a direction. Visualize a group of five people who have formed a line by holding hands. The first person in line uses his left hand to hold the right hand of the next person in line. The second person uses her left hand to hold the right hand of the third person in line, and so on. Therefore, the line has a direction. The person at one end of the line has a free left hand and the person at the other end has a free right hand.

Remember that a nucleotide has a deoxyribose sugar molecule, a chemical group that contains phosphorus, and a base. The sugar group of one nucleotide binds with the phosphorous group of another nucleotide to form the sugar-phosphate backbone of DNA.

Each sugar molecule has five carbon atoms, numbered 1 to 5. In a nucleotide, the phosphorous group is attached to carbon number 5. To create the sugar-phosphate backbone, a bond is formed between the number 3 carbon in the sugar of one nucleotide and the phosphorous group of the next nucleotide.

Think about a very short piece of DNA that has only five nucleotides. For convenience, "P" represents the phosphorous group. The symbol "5-sugar-3" stands for a sugar molecule's number 5 and number 3 carbons. "P– 5-sugar-3" represents a sugar molecule with a phosphorous group attached to the number 5 carbon. The sugar-phosphate backbone can be drawn as follows:

P – 5-sugar-3 – P – 5-sugar-3 – P – 5-sugar-3 – P – 5-sugar-3 – P – 5-sugar-3

Notice that the sugar-phosphate backbone has one end with a number 5 carbon carrying a phosphorous group that is not bound to another nucleotide. At the other end, a number 3 carbon is not bound to another nucleotide. Just like a line of people, a DNA molecule has a direction.

In the diagram of a short piece of DNA shown below, the number 5 carbon's free phosphorous group appears on the left and the free number 3 carbon appears on the right.

P– 5------------------------3

Crick proposed that a DNA helix contains two DNA molecules, and that the molecules run in opposite directions. The two molecules can be diagramed as shown below:

P– 5------------------------3

3------------------------5– P

Watson and Crick built another model of DNA. This one was a double-stranded helix with DNA molecules that ran in opposite directions. Using cardboard cutouts of bases, Watson found that an adenine on one DNA strand fit with a thymine on the other DNA strand, and that a guanine on one strand fit with a cytosine on the other.

Watson had discovered the rules of the attraction between the bases of the nucleotides. An A on one DNA strand pairs with a T on the other DNA strand, and a G on one DNA strand pairs with a C on the other DNA strand. This attraction between pairs of bases can be imagined as a type of magnetic attraction. The attraction between **base pairs** explains why two molecules of DNA stay together. The presence of base pairs also explains why Erwin Chargaff found that DNA contains equal amounts of adenine and thymine bases, and equal amounts of cytosine and guanine bases.

Consider a very short DNA molecule with two strands. One strand has the following sequence: CATTAGCATGGACT. The other strand would have the sequence GTAATCGTACCTGA. Together, the strands would appear as follows:

CATTAGCATGGACT

GTAATCGTACCTGA

This is the case because the first C in CATTAGCATGGACT pairs with the first G in GTAATCGTACCTGA, the first A in CATTAG-CATGGACT pairs with the first T in GTAATCGTACCTGA, and so on.

When paired, the base pairs, AT and GC, have the same overall shape. Since they have the same shape, an AT base pair and a GC base pair can fit into any order between the two sugar-phosphate backbones without deforming the helix. The order of the nucleotides in a DNA molecule can carry a complex genetic code.

RNA: GENETIC CODE MESSENGER

Watson and Crick's 1953 paper on the DNA double helix grabbed the notice of George Gamow, a famous astronomer and physicist. Gamow had been born in Russia and moved to the United States in 1934. He made great contributions in physics and astronomy, including the advancement of the Big Bang Theory, the theory about the origin of our universe. But the idea of a DNA helix inspired Gamow to venture into the field of genetics.

Gamow pointed out that the DNA helix has diamond-shaped holes formed by four bases. Mixtures of the four types of bases in the helix produced 20 different types of holes. The number of common amino acids also happens to be 20. Gamow suggested that amino acids bound to certain holes, and then amino acids linked together to form a protein.

Scientists noted several problems with this "diamond code." For example, Gamow's model required that protein synthesis must take place on DNA, which is located in a cell's nucleus. Yet recent studies showed that protein synthesis occurred in the cytoplasm, not in the nucleus.

How did a cell transfer genetic code data stored in DNA to protein production machinery in the cytoplasm? Scientists proposed that ribonucleic acid (RNA) molecules carried this information.

An RNA molecule is similar to a DNA molecule, but RNA and DNA differ in three ways. First, RNA has a base called uracil that takes the place of thymine in DNA. For example, the sequence AGA TGT CCT in a piece of DNA would appear as AGA UGU CCU in an RNA molecule. Another difference between DNA and RNA is that DNA contains *deoxyribose* sugars, whereas RNA contains *ribose* sugars. This is why one is called DNA and the other is called RNA. A third difference concerns the structure of RNA and DNA. RNA usually exists in the form of a single strand, whereas DNA can be found as a double helix.

The type of RNA molecule that transfers DNA's information to the protein-making machinery is called **messenger RNA** (mRNA). Messenger RNA has a nucleotide sequence that is a copy of a nucleotide sequence found in a DNA molecule. Of course, a messenger RNA molecule will not carry an exact copy of a DNA molecule's nucleotide sequence. DNA uses thymine, whereas RNA uses uracil.

After scientists understood that messenger RNA shuttles genetic data from the nucleus to the cytoplasm, they focused on RNA and its nucleotides. A race began among scientists to be the first to crack the genetic code.

THE GENETIC CODE REVEALED

Scientists used the following clues to crack the genetic code:

- One gene is responsible for the synthesis of one protein.
- Genes are located in DNA.
- Nucleotide sequences in the DNA double helix encode amino acid sequences in proteins.
- Messenger RNA carries genetic code information to protein synthesis machinery.

Another clue about the genetic code came from mathematics. Since RNA contains only four different types of bases and proteins contain 20 common types of amino acids, a single base does not code for a single amino acid. Suppose that the code used combinations of two bases to signal one type of amino acid. In that case, the bases could code for only 16 different amino acids (4 x 4). If the genetic code used mixtures of three bases to code for an amino acid, then the bases would provide 64 combinations (4 x 4 x 4). This is more than enough to encode the 20 amino acids. A triplet code, therefore, would be the simplest type of code.

At the National Institutes of Health in Maryland, scientist Marshall Nirenberg decided to examine how RNA controlled protein

synthesis. In 1961, Nirenberg and Heinrich Matthaei, a fellow researcher, ground bacteria to create a mixture that could make proteins. They divided a bacterial mix into 20 test tubes and added one
type of amino acid to each. In these experiments, one test tube contained an amino acid that had been radioactively tagged, and 19 test
tubes contained amino acids that had not been tagged.

To produce a messenger RNA, they made a polymer of uracil
referred to as "poly-U." Poly-U had the form of UUUUUUUUUU
[. . . .] In one experiment, they tagged the amino acid phenylalanine,
or "Phe." When they added poly-U to the bacterial mixtures, the
protein synthesis machinery made a radioactive protein. The protein

Does the Genetic Code Overlap Itself?

Before cracking the genetic code, scientists tackled a key
question: Does the code overlap?

An overlapping code can be easily pictured. Think about
a piece of RNA with the nucleotide sequence GAUGCUUGU.
If the code overlapped, then this sequence could contain
seven triplets that encode seven amino acids.

```
GAUGCUUGU
GAU
 AUG
  UGC
   GCU
    CUU
     UUG
      UGU
```

If the code did not overlap, then the sequence would
contain three triplets that encode three amino acids: GAU
GCU UGU.

Studies on genetic mutants in viruses provided clues
about whether the genetic code overlapped. One finding

was a Phe polymer. They had cracked the first word of the genetic code. "UUU" caused the addition of Phe to a make a protein.

In another experiment, the scientists added a polymer of cytosine, or CCCCCCCCCC [. . .] to the bacterial protein-making brew. This time, the protein was a polymer of the amino acid proline. So, CCC codes for proline. Similar experiments revealed that AAA codes for lysine and GGG encodes for glycine.

Har Gobind Khorana, a scientist at the University of Wisconsin, Madison, invented a way to make RNA polymers that contained more than one base. He used these synthetic messenger RNA molecules to make proteins that had two or more amino acids. Khorana's

was that a single base change could alter a single amino acid in a protein. Does this finding suggest a code that overlaps or a code that does not overlap?

Suppose that the first uracil in the sequence GAUGCUUGU becomes mutated to a cytosine. The altered sequence would be GACGCUUGU. If the code overlapped, then the triplets would appear as follows:

```
GACGCUUGU
GAC
 ACG
  CGC
   GCU
    CUU
     UUG
      UGU
```

A single mutation changes three triplets that code for amino acids.

What would happen if the code does not overlap? Then, a single change in GAC GCU UGU would change the coding sequence for only one amino acid. This result agrees with observations of genetic mutants. Other studies confirmed that the genetic code is not an overlapping code.

experiments revealed more of the genetic code. The studies also confirmed that the genetic code is based upon triplets of bases. A triplet of bases is known as a **codon**.

By 1966, scientists had decoded all of the genetic code's codons. They found that not all base triplets instruct a cell to add an amino acid. Certain triplets of bases instruct the cell's protein-making machinery to start or to stop protein synthesis. Researchers began to realize that the genetic code is a data transfer system as complex as a code that might be used by a spy.

The Genetic Code at Work: Gene Expression

I n 1957, Francis Crick proposed that genetic data moves in only one direction. That is, genetic data transmits from DNA to RNA to protein. After genetic information has passed into protein, the information stays there: It cannot transfer back into RNA or DNA. Since 1957, scientists have found a number of exceptions to this rule. For instance, certain viruses contain RNA as their nucleic acid molecule. RNA viruses have an enzyme that can make DNA by copying the nucleotide sequence in the RNA molecule, a process that reverses the flow of genetic information. So far, scientists have not observed a transfer of information from protein back to RNA.

The transfer of nucleotide sequence data would accomplish nothing if it were not for the genetic code. The code enables cells to make proteins, form tissues, and sustain an organism's life.

FEATURES OF THE GENETIC CODE

Scientists cracked the genetic code using crushed bacterial cells to make proteins. Animal cells use the same genetic code discovered in bacteria. In fact, almost all life on Earth has the same genetic code.

The genetic code is based on triplets—codons—of the four nucleotide bases found in RNA: adenine, guanine, cytosine, and uracil. A coding system based upon a series of three of four possible bases yields 64 possible combinations (4 x 4 x 4). Cells use all 64 codons, and yet, there are only 20 common amino acids. Some amino acids are encoded by two or more codons. For example, the amino acid leucine is encoded by the codons UUA, UUG, CUU, CUA, CUC, and CUG. Since some amino acids are encoded by more than one nucleotide triplet, scientists say that the genetic code is degenerate.

Not all codons stand for an amino acid; some codons act like start and stop signals. Consider the following nucleotide sequence in a very small messenger RNA molecule:

... GCAAGGCCGAUGGGGCGAAUUGCAUGCCCGUGA ...

How should a cell's protein synthesis machinery read the sequence as triplets? There are three possibilities:

...GCA AGG CCG AUG GGG CGA AUU GCA UGC CCG UGA...

...G CAA GGC CGA UGG GGC GAA UUG CAU GCC CGU GA...

...GC AAG GCC GAU GGG GCG AAU UGC AUG CCC GUG A...

The codon AUG encodes the amino acid methionine. AUG also signals the place in the nucleotide sequence of an mRNA where the code for a protein begins. The AUG codon creates the **reading frame** for the nucleotide sequence and determines how the sequence should be grouped into triplets. In the example, an AUG resides at nucleotides 10 to 12:

... GCAAGGCCGAUGGGGCGAAUUGCAUGCCCGUGA ...

The AUG codon signals that the nucleotide sequence should be read as:

AUG GGG CGA AUU GCA UGC CCG UGA

Not every protein has a methionine amino acid at one end. The amino acid may be removed after protein synthesis has finished.

The genetic code signals the end of protein synthesis with a stop codon. In the example above, a UGA codon signals the end of a

Genetic Code

Second letter

		U	C	A	G	
First letter	**U**	UUU Phenyl- UUC alanine UUA Leucine UUG	UCU UCC UCA Serine UCG	UAU Tyrosine UAC UAA Stop codon UAG Stop codon	UGU Cysteine UGC UGA Stop codon UGG Tryptophan	U C A G
	C	CUU CUC Leucine CUA CUG	CCU CCC Proline CCA CCG	CAU Histidine CAC CAA Glutamine CAG	CGU CGC Arginine CGA CGG	U C A G
	A	AUU AUC Isoleucine AUA AUG Methionine	ACU ACC Threonine ACA ACG	AAU Asparagine AAC AAA Lysine AAG	AGU Serine AGC AGA Arginine AGG	U C A G
	G	GUU GUC Valine GUA GUG	GCU GCC Alanine GCA GCG	GAU Aspartic GAC acid GAA Glutamic GAG acid	GGU GGC Glycine GGA GGG	U C A G

Third letter

Figure 4.1 This table provides a visual guide to how different combinations of the four nucleotides in DNA direct the formation of different amino acids.

protein-encoding nucleotide sequence. UAA and UAG are also stop codons. Sometimes, the stop codons are referred to as "nonsense codons" as they code for nothing.

PROTEIN SYNTHESIS

Transcription

Cells can be classified into two basic types: prokaryotic and eukaryotic. A **prokaryotic** cell, such as a bacterium, lacks a nucleus. Animal cells and other **eukaryotic** cells have a nucleus. In both types of cells, the process of protein synthesis begins with the conversion of DNA-encoded genetic data to its RNA equivalent. The synthesis of an RNA molecule from a DNA template is called **transcription**. In prokaryotes, the RNA transcript serves as messenger RNA (mRNA).

Eukaryotic cells have a more complex and interesting way to use the RNA transcript.

The nuclei of eukaryotic cells contain a lot of DNA that does not encode proteins. In humans, protein-encoded DNA amounts to

The Caesar Cipher

In 46 B.C., Julius Caesar became ruler of the Roman Empire. Before he seized power, Caesar had waged successful battles in Western Europe and greatly extended Rome's territory. Caesar devised a secret method of writing to keep in touch with his army's leaders. It was one of the earliest and simplest forms of encryption.

To encrypt a message, a writer substitutes letters of the everyday, plain alphabet for letters or symbols in a cipher alphabet. Julius Caesar created a cipher alphabet by replacing each letter in his message with the letter found three places to the right in the plain alphabet. Using the first 12 letters of the modern English alphabet, for example, the plain alphabet and Caesar's cipher alphabet appear as follows:

Plain: ABCD EFGH IJKL
Cipher: DEFG HIJK LMNO

In the cipher alphabet, the series of letters has been shifted by three. Knowing about the three letter shift, a person can convert the cipher text message "FURVV WKH ULYHU QRZ" to the plaintext message "Cross the river now." An enemy who intercepted one of Caesar's encrypted messages would not be able to read it. Only Caesar and his generals knew about the cipher alphabet.

Today, this encryption method is known as the Caesar shift cipher or Caesar cipher. By modern standards, Caesar's substitution cipher offers very weak cryptography. Plastic decoder rings—popular cereal box trinkets at one time—employ substitution ciphers.

about 2% of total DNA in a cell. Some of the noncoding DNA can be found in the middle of nucleotide sequences that encode a protein. As a result, a gene that encodes a protein has two types of DNA: **exons** (expressed regions), which are areas of DNA that encode parts of a protein; and **introns** (intervening regions), which are pieces of DNA that do not encode parts of a protein. A simple gene may have a structure, such as:

[exon] – [intron] – [exon] – [intron] – [exon] – [intron] – [exon]

In eukaryotic cells, transcription produces a pre-mRNA transcript that must be processed into mRNA. A vital part of the process is RNA splicing. During RNA splicing, introns are cleaved from pre-mRNA and exons are spliced together to produce an RNA molecule with a continuous stretch of protein-coding nucleotide sequences. The process of RNA splicing must be accurate. An error that adds or deletes just one nucleotide disrupts the nucleotide sequence that encodes a protein. Such an error can block protein synthesis or result in the synthesis of a mutant protein.

Scientists have proposed a reason to explain why eukaryotic cells have such complex gene structures. The exon-intron arrangement allows cells to make different proteins by stitching together different combinations of exons during RNA splicing. The mixing of exons in diverse patterns is called alternative splicing. In an extreme example, transcription of the fruit fly DSCAM gene can produce pre-mRNA with 119 exons. RNA splicing reduces the number of exons to 17. Shuffling fruit fly DSCAM gene exons can theoretically produce over 38,000 different proteins.

Alternative splicing explains a surprising discovery about human DNA. Human cells can make hundreds of thousands of different proteins. Yet human DNA contains only about 20,000 protein-encoding genes. Cells need fewer genes when RNA splicing can make different mRNAs from the same pre-mRNA.

Translation

The next step of protein synthesis is called **translation**. In effect, genetic code data in an mRNA molecule is translated into a sequence of amino acids in a protein. In eukaryotes, this step occurs after mature, spliced mRNA leaves the nucleus and enters the cytoplasm.

In the mid-1950s, Francis Crick proposed a theory about protein synthesis. It seemed highly unlikely, he said, that amino acids specifically bind with mRNA bases that encoded the amino acid. Rather, adaptor molecules—probably small RNA molecules—brought the correct amino acids together by binding an amino acid and its matching codon in mRNA. Crick was correct. The adaptor molecules are short, single-stranded RNAs called **transfer RNAs** (tRNAs).

One end of a tRNA molecule has an **anticodon**—three nucleotides that can form base pairs with a codon in mRNA. At its other end, the tRNA carries an amino acid specified by the mRNA codon. A tRNA that carries its specified amino acid is often called a "charged tRNA." Each tRNA can bind one specific type of amino acid. Therefore, a cell must contain at least one tRNA for each of the 20 common amino acids. Enzymes known as *tRNA transferases* recognize the unique features of a tRNA and attach the correct amino acid. These enzymes are the key to the transfer of genetic data in protein synthesis. They read the language of the genetic code found at one end of a tRNA and match the code to a specific amino acid.

The genetic code has 61 nucleotide triplets that code for amino acids. Thanks to an effect known as **wobble**, a cell does not have to contain 61 types of tRNAs. The wobble effect works like this: Certain amino acids are encoded by four codons that differ by only one nucleotide. The amino acid alanine, for example, is encoded by GCA, GCC, GCG, and GCU. For alanine, the third nucleotide of the codon adds nothing to the codon's specificity. That is, alanine is encoded by GCx, where x is any of the four nucleotides. There is a wobble at the third position. A single tRNA charged with alanine may recognize some or all of the four codons for alanine.

An mRNA molecule and charged tRNAs meet at ribosomes. A **ribosome**, which is composed of RNA and protein, recognizes the signal in mRNA for the start of translation. Ribosomes stabilize interactions between mRNA and charged tRNAs and supply enzymatic activity that links amino acids from the tRNAs to form a protein. Ribosomes move along an mRNA, exposing codons of an mRNA one by one to ensure a correct addition of amino acids. After ribosomes reach a stop codon, they detach from the mRNA and the new protein.

Transfer RNA

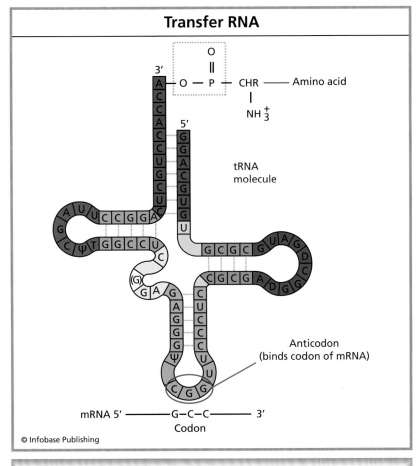

© Infobase Publishing

Figure 4.2 Transfer RNA is involved in protein synthesis. It is a small RNA molecule that transfers the correct active amino acid to a growing polypeptide chain at the ribosomal site of protein synthesis during translation.

AMINO ACIDS AND PROTEIN SHAPE

Protein synthesis can be imagined as adding amino acid "cars" to a growing protein polymer "train." However, a protein does not have the form of a linear train. Amino acids push and pull a protein into a shape. For example, a protein can have a spiral shape, the shape of a knot, or a combination of these shapes.

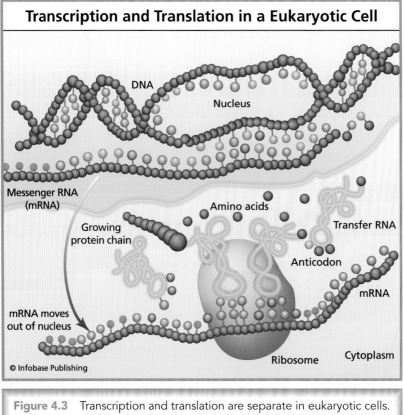

Transcription and Translation in a Eukaryotic Cell

DNA

Nucleus

Messenger RNA
(mRNA)

Amino acids

Transfer RNA

Growing
protein chain

Anticodon

mRNA

mRNA moves
out of nucleus

Ribosome

Cytoplasm

© Infobase Publishing

Figure 4.3 Transcription and translation are separate in eukaryotic cells. Transcription occurs in the nucleus to produce a pre-mRNA molecule. This molecule is typically processed to produce mature mRNA, which exists in the nucleus and is translated in the cytoplasm.

Each of the 20 amino acids has two basic components. One part, which is the same in all amino acids, allows amino acids to couple with each other like train cars. The other part—a side group—differs among the amino acids. One way to picture a protein is to imagine the identical parts of amino acids forming a chain. Each amino acid has a side group that sticks out from the chain.

Because of the different side groups, the sequence of amino acids determines a protein's shape in the watery environment of a cell. Some side groups are **hydrophobic** ("water-fearing"). These move away from water and toward a protein's dry interior. Hydrophobic groups act like the head of scared turtle, ducking inside the shell.

Other side groups are **hydrophilic** ("water-loving"). These side groups move away from the protein's interior to the watery exterior of a protein. Other side groups are attracted to each other and bend the protein to move parts of the chain closer together.

Amino acid side groups are like a pack of bratty children. They all want something and will do what is needed to get their way. As amino acid side groups move to get their way, they bend and fold the protein. Their combined activities determine a protein's shape. The shape of a protein is critical in determining the protein's function.

A protein may have four types of structure that determine its final shape:

- The **primary structure** of a protein is the sequence of amino acids in the protein polymer.
- The **secondary structure** occurs when a protein's amino acids become linked by weak chemical bonds involving hydrogen atoms. Hydrogen bonds can pull one or more sections of a protein chain into the spiral shape of an alpha-helix or into a kinked structure, known as a beta-pleated sheet.
- The **tertiary structure** is formed as amino acid side groups bend, twist, and fold the protein into a complex three-dimensional shape.
- Some proteins have a **quaternary structure**. This simply means that an active protein molecule contains two or more protein subunits. A protein may have a number of identical subunits or a collection of different subunits.

The sequence of codons in a protein's gene determines the primary structure. In turn, the sequence of amino acids in a protein determines secondary structure, tertiary structure, and the way that protein subunits interact to form a quaternary structure.

GENE MUTATIONS AND THE GENETIC CODE

A gene mutation—a change in a gene's nucleotide sequence—can take many forms. Some mutations are caused by a single base change, while others are caused by a massive alteration in a chromosome that

Types of Protein Structures

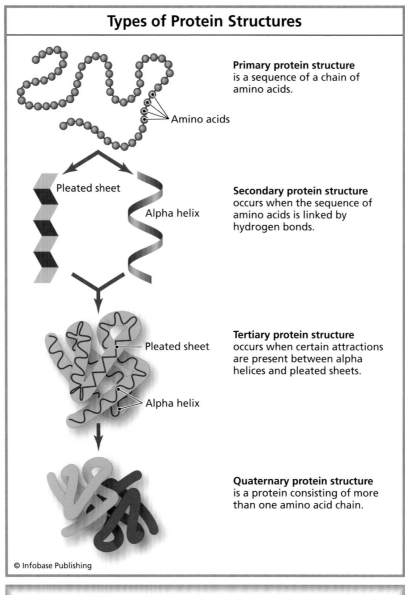

Primary protein structure is a sequence of a chain of amino acids.

Amino acids

Pleated sheet

Alpha helix

Secondary protein structure occurs when the sequence of amino acids is linked by hydrogen bonds.

Pleated sheet

Alpha helix

Tertiary protein structure occurs when certain attractions are present between alpha helices and pleated sheets.

Quaternary protein structure is a protein consisting of more than one amino acid chain.

© Infobase Publishing

Figure 4.4 There are four types of protein structures. All proteins have a primary, secondary, and tertiary structure. Some have a quaternary structure as well.

can be seen under a microscope. A gene mutation can be inherited; parents can pass on mutations to their offspring. Gene mutations can also accumulate during an organism's lifetime. Environmental factors, such as certain chemicals and the sun's ultraviolet light, can mutate DNA. A mutation can also occur from an error created when DNA duplicates itself before cell division. Unless an organism's gametes carry a mutation, the mutation will not be passed on to offspring.

The addition or deletion of nucleotides can create a **frameshift mutation**. As the name suggests, this type of mutation changes the reading frame of a nucleotide sequence that encodes protein. By shifting the way that mRNA bases are grouped into three, the mutation alters the series of amino acids. Consider the following short piece of mRNA that encodes the amino acid sequence leucine-valine-alanine-glutamine: CUU GUU GCU CAA. Suppose that a mutation in DNA results in the loss of the first uracil in the mRNA. The reading frame shifts to CUG UUG CUC AA. The new sequence encodes leucine-leucine-leucine with two adenine bases left over. Suppose that a mutation caused the addition of guanine next to the first guanine in the sequence. The mutated sequence would be grouped as CUU GGU UGC UCA A and would encode leucine-glycine-cysteine-serine with an adenine left over.

Here is a strange thing about mutations: Sometimes, more is better. An insertion of a base corrects the reading frame for a deletion of a base, just as a deletion corrects the reading frame for an insertion. Consider the following sequence:

UUA GUC UCU ACU GCU GAA GAG CAA AAU GGU AGU

Then suppose that a mutation causes the loss of the last uracil in the third codon:

UUA GUC UCU̶ ACU GCU GAA GAG CAA AAU GGU AGU

A frameshift would occur as follows with mutated codons shown in red:

UUA GUC UCA CUG CUG AAG AGC AAA AUG GUA GU.

Now, suppose that the gene experienced two mutations: the loss of the last uracil in the third codon and the addition of an adenine in the fifth codon:

UUA GUC UCU̶ ACU GACU GAA GAG CAA AAU GGU AGU

The mutated sequence would be read as follows with the mutated codons shown in red:

UUA GUC UCA CUG ACU GAA GAG CAA AAU GGU AGU

The second mutation decreased the effects of the first mutation. Two mutations of opposite type—an insertion and a deletion—limit the effects of mutation on the reading frame.

Multiple mutations of the same type can also limit the result of gene mutation. For example, three insertions or multiples of three insertions may correct the reading frame for the majority of the encoded amino acids. This is true because the addition of every three nucleotides adds one amino acid to the protein. The rule of three also applies to nucleotide deletions. In these cases, the mutations cause the loss of one or more amino acids.

Mutations not only cause the loss or gain of a nucleotide; a mutation can also replace one nucleotide with another. A nucleotide replacement, also called a **point mutation**, can affect a codon in one of three ways.

In a **silent mutation**, the mutated codon still encodes the same amino acid. For instance, the mutation of CAA to CAG does not affect the amino acid added to a protein; both codons encode the amino acid glutamine. Silent mutations can exist because the genetic code is degenerate.

In a **nonsense mutation**, the mutation creates a stop codon from a codon that encoded an amino acid. The mutation of CAA to UAA is a nonsense mutation. Since protein synthesis stops too early, a nonsense mutation results in a shortened protein. The short protein may not function or may function poorly.

In a **missense mutation**, the mutation alters a codon for one amino acid to a codon for a different amino acid. For example, the mutation of CAA to GAA would replace glutamine with glutamic acid.

A missense mutation can greatly affect the function of a protein. In turn, an altered protein can deeply affect a person's health. Consider a mutation in the gene that encodes **hemoglobin**, the protein that carries oxygen in red blood cells. Hemoglobin has a quaternary structure: The protein has two alpha-globin subunits and two beta-globin subunits. One type of missense mutation alters the sixth codon of a beta-globin gene, so that the mRNA has a GUG codon rather than a GAG codon. As a result, the mutated beta-globin has the amino acid valine instead of glutamic acid. This mutation can be

A Mutant Virus

The West Nile virus was first identified over 70 years ago by researchers in Africa. The virus infects birds. Mosquitoes that bite infected birds get the virus and then infect other birds. Sometimes, the mosquitoes infect humans and cause a mild fever. The West Nile virus became more deadly to humans during the mid-1990s when it caused serious brain infections in people living in Europe, Russia, and North Africa.

In 1999, researchers detected the West Nile virus in North America. The virus infected humans, birds, and other animals. During 2007 in the United States, 43 states reported more than 3,500 cases of human West Nile virus illness; 124 of these cases proved fatal. More than 2,000 dead birds suffering from West Nile virus infection were reported in 35 states.

Scientists have studied how the virus could turn so deadly. In 2007, one group reported on their examination of the genes of 21 types of West Nile virus. They found a gene mutation that caused a change of a single amino acid. The mutation had occurred three different times; each time, the mutated virus was associated with outbreaks of human disease.

The scientists investigated the mutation in the lab. In one experiment, they inoculated crows with two types of West Nile virus; one type of the virus had the mutation and the other did not. Two to three days after exposure to the non-mutant virus, the crows' blood carried detectable amounts of viruses. By the third day of infection with the deadly mutant virus, the scientists found 10,000 times the number of viruses swarming in the blood of these crows.

The amino acid mutation occurs in helicase, an enzyme needed for the West Nile virus to reproduce itself. The mutant helicase enables the virus to multiply at high rates. A helicase mutation can explain why scientists found an increased number of mutant viruses in the blood of infected crows.

found in the altered hemoglobin beta-globins of a person who has sickle cell anemia.

A single amino acid replacement causes the symptoms of sickle cell anemia because valine and glutamic acid have different chemical properties. Valine is hydrophobic, whereas glutamic acid is hydrophilic. Sickle cell hemoglobin molecules bind with each other as hydrophobic valine of one beta-globin subunit seeks out a dry region in another beta-globin subunit. The mutated hemoglobins polymerize to long, rigid rope-like structures.

In sickle cell anemia, polymerized hemoglobin molecules distort the shape of red blood cells. Hemoglobin polymers stretch the cells into long, crescent-like forms. These sickle-shaped red blood cells cling to blood vessel walls and block blood flow. The stress caused by the formation of hemoglobin polymers reduces the life span of red blood cells. The increased destruction of red blood cells results in anemia, which is a shortage of red blood cells.

Using the Genetic Code to Transform Living Things

GENETIC ENGINEERING

During the 1950s, scientists discovered the DNA double helix. The 1960s brought an understanding about how cells use genetic data in DNA to make proteins. Scientists learned how life on Earth uses the genetic code. During the 1970s, scientists began to use the genetic code to produce new molecules and altered life forms. This decade marked the launch of genetic engineering.

Tools of the Genetic Engineer

The word "engineering" refers to the use of science to design and to construct things. Genetic engineering involves using science to isolate, analyze, and modify genes. Scientists who work in this field also transfer genes from one organism to another. The transferred gene is often called a **transgene**, while an organism that receives a transgene may be called a **transgenic** organism or a genetically engineered organism. Genetic engineering relies upon **recombinant DNA** technology. Recombinant DNA is DNA that has been altered in the laboratory by the addition or deletion of nucleotide sequences.

Scientists transfer genes by the application of three techniques. One technique is a method for identifying a gene's nucleotide sequence. Methods for sequencing nucleic acids were available before 1970. Although they worked, the methods were tedious and slow. Quick sequencing techniques were developed around the mid-1970s and enabled rapid advances in genetic engineering.

Gene transfer also requires a method for cutting and pasting a gene with other DNA molecules. In 1969, American scientist Hamilton O. Smith discovered that bacteria make enzymes—called **restriction enzymes**—that cut DNA at specific places. A restriction enzyme glides along the backbone of a DNA molecule until it comes across a certain target nucleotide sequence that is called its cleavage site. There, the enzyme binds to the DNA molecule. Once the enzyme has the DNA backbone in its firm grasp, the enzyme twists into a different shape. As the enzyme contorts, it distorts the DNA molecule and breaks the DNA backbone. Different restriction enzymes bind to different cleavage sites. By using a collection of various restriction enzymes, a genetic engineer can cleave DNA at selected places.

A third technique required for gene transfer is a system for transporting a transgene into an organism. One system was discovered in November 1972 when scientists met in Hawaii to discuss **plasmids**, which are small, circular DNA molecules that replicate themselves in bacterial cells and can transfer from one bacterial cell to another. Stanley Cohen, a scientist at Stanford University in California and who was attending the Hawaii meeting, listened to a lecture on restriction enzymes by Herbert Boyer of the University of California, San Francisco. Over dinner at a deli, the two scientists agreed to combine their knowledge of plasmids and restriction enzymes.

Cohen, Boyer, and their associates altered plasmids to deliver a transgene into a bacterial cell. A plasmid, or similar DNA molecule, that is used to transfer DNA into a cell is called a **vector**. The scientists published three papers on recombinant DNA technology in 1973 and 1974. In one study, they inserted ribosomal RNA genes from a frog into a plasmid and transformed *Escherichia coli* bacteria with the modified plasmid. Then, they isolated RNA from the *E. coli*

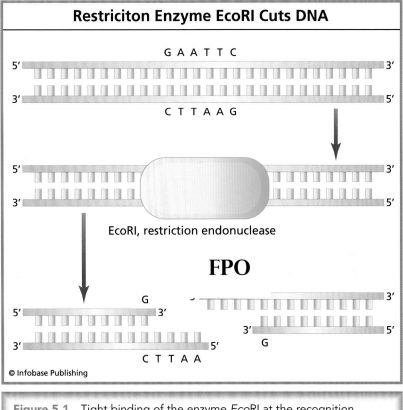

Restriciton Enzyme EcoRI Cuts DNA

EcoRI, restriction endonuclease

FPO

© Infobase Publishing

Figure 5.1 Tight binding of the enzyme *Eco*RI at the recognition site causes its structure to change, bringing the parts of the enzyme necessary for DNA cleavage closer to the DNA strand. Then, the "backbone" of the DNA molecule can be broken to produce two DNA fragments.

bacteria and found that the bacteria had produced ribosomal RNA from the frog genes. The frog transgenes functioned in the bacteria.

The researchers cut and pasted their vector using the restriction enzyme *Eco*RI. This enzyme seeks out the nucleotide sequence GAATTC. *Eco*RI breaks a DNA molecule after the guanine (G) nucleotide in the cleavage site. In a double-stranded DNA molecule, the cleavage site would appear as follows:

. . . . GAATTC . . . .

. . . . CTTAAG . . . .

In the Cohen-Boyer study, *Eco*RI cut open a circular plasmid. Cleavage of the DNA left two short stubs of single-stranded DNA, called "sticky ends." Sticky ends can form base pairs with themselves or with matching pieces of DNA.

. . . . G   AATTC . . . .

. . . . CTTAA   G . . . .

*Eco*RI then cut the frog ribosomal genes at both ends, creating two sticky ends.

AATTC . . . . G

G . . . . CTTAA

After mixing the cleaved plasmid and frog genes, the two types of DNA fit together like pieces of a puzzle by forming base pairs at the sticky ends.

. . . . GAATTC . . . . GAATTC . . . .

. . . . CTTAAG . . . . CTTAAG . . . .

An enzyme called **ligase** sealed the breaks in the DNA molecules. Restriction enzymes are like scissors and ligase enzymes are like glue.

The Cohen and Boyer experiments formed the foundation of the basic genetic engineering process:

- Cleave a gene from chromosomal DNA with restriction enzymes.
- Splice the gene into a plasmid or other vector.
- Insert the vector into a host cell to produce a transgenic cell.
- Culture transgenic cells that produce copies of the vector.

The ability to insert a transgene into bacteria has great commercial value. Bacteria make efficient protein factories because bacteria reproduce at a very fast rate, as rapid as once about every 20 minutes. A bacterial cell reproduces by splitting into two cells. Each of these split into two cells, creating four cells. The four cells split to form eight cells, which split to create 16 cells, which split to form 32 cells, and so on. In this way, one *E. coli* cell can produce about

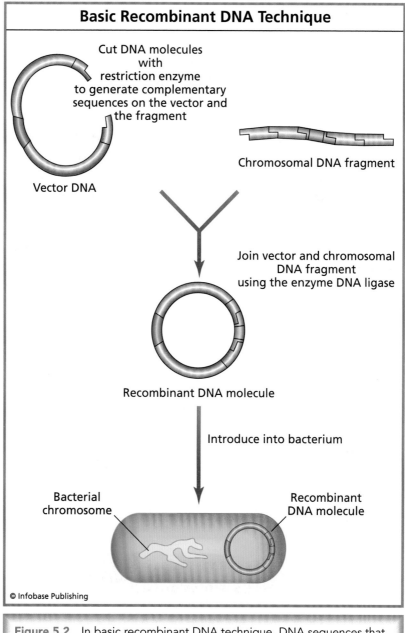

Basic Recombinant DNA Technique

Cut DNA molecules with restriction enzyme to generate complementary sequences on the vector and the fragment

Chromosomal DNA fragment

Vector DNA

Join vector and chromosomal DNA fragment using the enzyme DNA ligase

Recombinant DNA molecule

Introduce into bacterium

Bacterial chromosome

Recombinant DNA molecule

© Infobase Publishing

Figure 5.2 In basic recombinant DNA technique, DNA sequences that would not normally occur together are combined.

17 million offspring cells during an eight-hour period. If the parent *E. coli* carries a transgene, then its offspring also should carry copies of the transgene and make proteins encoded by the transgene.

Today, proteins used in medicine and in industry are produced in fermentation vessels that hold thousands of gallons of transgenic *E. coli.* Transgenic yeast cells and transgenic mammalian cells are also used to make proteins.

Scientists not only use recombinant DNA technology to produce proteins found in nature, but also to make new proteins. For example, scientists used DNA technology to alter subtilisin, a protein-digesting enzyme that is used in laundry detergent. Normal subtilisin has a drawback for detergents in that bleach inactivates the enzyme. Researchers found that bleach affects the amino acid methionine at position 222 of the enzyme's amino acid sequence. So, they modified the genetic code of a subtilisin gene to replace methionine with the amino acid alanine. The resulting genetically-engineered subtilisin resists bleach inactivation. Scientists have also altered the subtilisin genetic code to produce enzymes that have improved stability at high temperatures.

Production of Insulin in Bacteria

In 1982, human insulin became the first genetic engineering product approved for **therapeutic** use in humans. Insulin is a protein hormone secreted into the bloodstream by an organ called the pancreas. The bloodstream carries insulin proteins to many types of cells where they bind to cell membranes. This binding changes the membrane to allow glucose to pass from the blood to the inside of the cell. (Cells use glucose as their main source of energy.)

Type 1 diabetes is a disease in which the pancreas no longer makes insulin. People who have this disorder cannot control the levels of glucose in their blood. To survive, a Type 1 diabetic must take insulin, usually by injection.

During the early 1920s, the first insulin was produced for diabetics. This insulin was isolated from the pancreases of pigs and cattle. Scientists continued their search for other sources of insulin. Finally, in the 1960s, researchers synthesized insulin protein. However, the process was not practical for large-scale production of the hormone. Genetic engineering soon offered another choice.

In pancreas cells, insulin is synthesized as a long "proinsulin" protein with three parts:

B chain – Connecting peptide (C peptide) – A chain

A **peptide** is simply an amino acid polymer that is shorter than a protein. The proinsulin protein is cleaved inside the cell to produce C peptide and mature insulin, which consists of the A and B chains joined by chemical bonds.

Scientists tried two tactics to produce bacteria that would synthesize human insulin. The first approach required two types of vectors: One vector had a nucleotide sequence that encoded the A chain and the other vector had a nucleotide sequence that encoded the B chain. The vectors were used to transform two separate batches of *E. coli* cells. After the A and B chains were isolated and purified from the bacteria brews, they were mixed to allow bonding between A chains and B chains.

In the second approach, scientists made a vector that included nucleotide sequences that encoded proinsulin and then transformed *E. coli* with the vector. Proinsulin was isolated from the bacterial brew, purified, and then converted into mature insulin hormone. This simpler tactic has become the preferred method. U.S. companies no longer make beef or pork insulin for medical use: Recombinant human insulin has become the standard medication.

The coding sequence of the human insulin gene had to be tweaked to get efficient production of the protein in *E. coli*. The tweaking was required because different types of organisms have preferences for one or more codons for a particular amino acid. The preference for codons is called **codon bias**. For example, six codons specify the amino acid arginine. The codon AGA encodes arginine about 22% of the time in human cells and about 1% of the time in *E. coli*. The bacteria may not produce enough of the tRNA that recognizes rarely used codons. This can impair the synthesis of proteins encoded by rare codons. To obtain higher yields of human insulin, the human insulin nucleotide sequence can be altered to contain codons preferred in *E. coli*. In the case of arginine, the codon can be changed to CGU, which *E. coli* cells use about 50% of the time.

Changing the nucleotide sequence of the insulin gene to adjust for codon bias does not alter insulin's amino acid sequence. However, scientists are changing the amino acid sequence of insulin to improve insulin treatment. For example, researchers have devised ways to reduce the tendency of human insulin molecules to bind together after injection. When insulin molecules bind with each other, it takes more time for insulin to reach the bloodstream. As a result, a diabetic may need to inject human insulin about 30 to 60 minutes before a meal, which can be inconvenient. One type of mutant insulin was made by switching two amino acids in the insulin B chain. Insulin molecules with the reversed amino acids are less likely to bind together and move more quickly to the bloodstream. Diabetics can inject one of these mutant quick-acting insulins immediately before a meal, which gives them more flexibility in their daily lives.

TRANSGENIC PLANTS

During the early 1980s, scientists devised a way to use a parasite to produce transgenic plants. In nature, a soil-dwelling bacteria, *Agrobacterium tumefaciens*, infects plant cells by inserting a plasmid into the plant's chromosomes. Scientists modified the plasmid into a vector that can be used to insert any gene into a plant cell.

Most plant cells are **totipotent**. This means that a complete plant can be grown from one plant cell. After treating plant cells with a vector, scientists culture the cells in plastic dishes in a laboratory. The cells are used to make a transgenic plant. If a transgenic plant produces viable seed, the transgene will be passed on to new generations.

A plasmid vector offers one way to make a transgenic plant. Another popular technique is called microprojectile bombardment, or **biolistics**—basically, this involves shooting DNA into a plant cell. The method is performed with DNA-coated gold particles that have diameters of about 0.000032 inches (0.8 microns). The particles are loaded into a gene gun and shot into plant cells at speeds up to 2,000 feet per second (600 meters per second). The first gene gun blasted DNA-coated pellets with gunpowder. Today, gene guns use high pressure helium gas to propel the particles. After DNA-coated particles burst through a plant cell wall, DNA is released from the particles and is inserted into chromosomes.

Techniques for making transgenic plants have been used extensively in agriculture. In 1996, farmers planted the first significant large-scale transgenic crop. Ten years later, farmers in 22 countries planted transgenic crops that covered over 252 million acres. Most of the crops were transgenic soybeans, corn, cotton, canola, and

Production of Transgenic Plants with Bacteria Genes

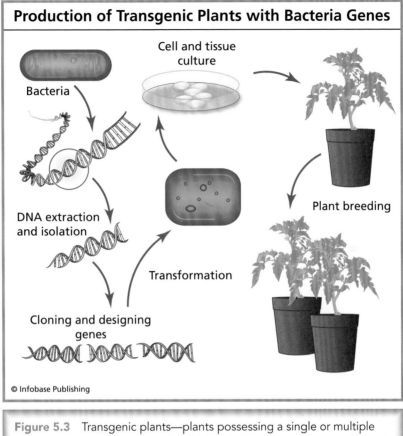

Cell and tissue culture

Bacteria

DNA extraction and isolation

Plant breeding

Transformation

Cloning and designing genes

© Infobase Publishing

Figure 5.3 Transgenic plants—plants possessing a single or multiple transgenes—can be produced with bacterial genes through recombinant DNA technology.

alfalfa. Farmers in the United States grew a little over half of the world's transgenic crops.

Many of the first transgenic crops produce proteins that kill insect pests. This eliminates the need for farmers to spray crops with traditional chemical **insecticides,** which are not only costly for farmers but also harmful to the environment. Chemical insecticides kill many North American species of birds, including peregrine falcons and bald eagles.

When scientists decided to make an insecticide-producing transgenic plant, they looked at a type of bacteria that lives in soil, *Bacillus thuringiensis.* The bacteria synthesize toxin proteins

("*Bt* toxins") that typically kill a limited number of insect species and do not directly affect other animals. The problem of codon bias cropped up in early experiments with *Bt* toxin genes. Compared with plant genes, *Bacillus* genes have a high adenine-plus-thymine content and a low guanine-plus-cytosine content. Scientists modified the bacterial codons to make them more suitable for plant cells.

The production of insecticidal protein is not the only trait that is added to transgenic crops. Certain transgenic plants can resist viruses that cause diseases and others have a transgene that allows the plant to survive **herbicide** treatment. One type of transgenic corn has a transgene that enables the plant to grow in land that has little water. Other transgenic plants have been designed for increased nutritional content and flavor.

Not all transgenic crops are grown for food. Some of them have been designed to synthesize proteins and chemicals for medicine

Golden Rice

Vitamin A is vital for a person's good health. Yet, the human body cannot make this vitamin, and so, humans must eat foods that contain beta-carotene, the chemical that gives a carrot its orange color. The human body then converts beta-carotene to Vitamin A. People risk Vitamin A shortage if they live on a diet with little beta-carotene. This can cause health problems, including blindness, severe infections, and life-threatening diseases.

Scientists invented one way to help people who have a Vitamin A deficiency: a transgenic rice called Golden Rice, which contains beta-carotene in the grain. Golden Rice contains two transgenes: One gene is obtained from a soil bacterium and the other is obtained from either daffodil or maize. The transgenes encode enzymes that work together to produce beta-carotene. With its yellow-orange color, Golden Rice stands out from ordinary white rice.

and industry. With molecular farming, or *biopharming*, transgenic plants can provide a means to produce therapeutic proteins and chemicals at lower cost and in greater amounts than traditional methods. For example, the French company Meristem Therapeutics grows transgenic corn plants that synthesize a form of a human enzyme called lipase. The enzyme can be used to treat people who have cystic fibrosis and other disorders that impair digestion.

TRANSGENIC ANIMALS

The December 16, 1982, issue of the journal *Nature* displayed a strange cover: a photo showing two mice from the same litter; one was normal while the other was a giant transgenic mouse. American scientists Richard Palmiter, Ralph Brinster, and their colleagues had injected a modified rat growth hormone gene into fertilized mouse

Figure 5.4   Golden rice (*right*) is shown opposite white rice. Golden rice is produced through genetic engineering to biosynthesize beta-carotene. It was first developed as a fortified food to be used in areas of the world where there is a shortage of vitamin A in people's diets.

eggs. The scientists then transferred the eggs into a mouse that acted as a foster mother. Although all of the pups had a normal size at birth, some of them rapidly grew to nearly twice the size of their litter mates. The birth of the so-called super mice marked the beginning of the production of transgenic animals. Since then, scientists have produced many transgenic mice, as well as transgenic fish, goats, sheep, chickens, cows, rabbits, and pigs.

To make their super mice, the Palmiter-Brinster team used the technique of DNA microinjection. The technique is performed by allowing a sperm cell to fuse with an egg cell. For a brief time, the

Smelling Yeast and Glowing Fish

Researchers at Temple University in Philadelphia, Pennsylvania, designed transgenic yeast that is used to sniff out the presence of explosives. This living detector was created by making transgenes that encode green **fluorescent** protein from jellyfish and proteins that are used by rats to sense odors. The rat proteins react to the presence of DNT, a substance that is chemically similar to the explosive TNT and causes the yeast cells to produce green fluorescent protein, which is visible under ultraviolet light. The scientists suggest that, one day, handheld sensors may contain cartridges filled with bomb-detecting transgenic yeast.

Some transgenic fish appear to glow, as well. In fact, scientists from the National University of Singapore invented a new way to detect water pollutants by producing transgenic zebra fish that emit a fluorescent glow when they contact certain impurities in the water. Typically, zebra fish are colored black and silver, but transgenic zebra fish have genes that encode proteins to produce fluorescence. The first transgenic fish radiated a red or green color due to the insertion of genes that were isolated from jellyfish. The scientists said that they could produce five types of zebra fish with this method. Each of these fish would glow in a different color in response to a different pollutant.

fused cell contains two **pronuclei**—one egg nucleus and one sperm cell nucleus. Then, the pronuclei combine to create one nucleus with a full set of chromosomes. Yet, before the two pronuclei fuse, a scientist injects a piece of DNA into one of the pronuclei. The DNA fragment, which includes one or more transgenes, inserts into the chromosomes. The pronuclei fuse and the cell continues to develop as an embryo. This remains a popular method for producing transgenic rats and mice.

Another popular method for making a transgenic animal requires a vector made from a virus. A normal virus carries the instructions

Figure 5.5   GloFish don't actually glow. They absorb and re-emit light so they appear to be glowing.

News about the glowing zebra fish stirred public interest. Many people wanted these unique animals for their home aquariums. Today, fish fans can buy GloFish fluorescent fish in red, orange, yellow, or green colors. While they appear brightly colored under white light, they seem to glow when illuminated with a **black light** in a dark room.

in its genetic material to reproduce itself, but lacks the means to do so. Instead, a virus must infect a cell and take over the cell's protein and nucleic acid synthesis machinery to make copies of itself. To construct a vector, scientists alter the virus's genetic material by removing genes for virus reproduction. Then, they add one or more transgenes. A virus vector can efficiently deliver transgenes to the chromosomes of young animal embryos.

Most transgenic animals are mice. Some transgenic mice are designed for research into basic questions of biology. Others provide animal models for the study of the causes of human diseases and possible treatments. The OncoMouse, for example, was produced by Harvard Medical School scientists to study the growth of cancers and to test cancer treatments. This mouse has a human transgene that causes the animal to be highly prone to develop cancer.

Scientists also use genetic engineering to alter livestock. Researchers have produced transgenic cows that synthesize protein-enriched milk, and transgenic pigs that provide more healthful types of meat. Other research efforts aim to produce transgenic livestock that resist diseases, such as mad cow disease.

Some transgenic pigs, goats, sheep, and cattle secrete protein drugs into their milk. The therapeutic proteins can be isolated from the milk, purified, and used as medicines for humans. In 2006, a European agency approved the medical use of human antithrombin protein that had been isolated from the milk of transgenic goats. Antithrombin, which inhibits blood clotting, can be used to treat a type of inherited disease in which a person lacks this crucial protein.

For more than 30 years, scientists have used recombinant DNA technology to manipulate nucleotide sequences that encode proteins. Transgenic bacteria, fungi, plants, and animals are the products of this technology. Recombinant DNA molecules have also been administered to humans as a treatment for an inherited disease. This is the field of **gene therapy**.

Genetic Variations That Affect Human Health

A person's **genome**—the genetic material that resides in the nuclei of a person's cells—controls many physical traits. Nucleotide sequences encode proteins for the color of the eyes, hair, and skin. Genes encode proteins that affect height and weight. A person's genome also has nucleotide sequences that can cause disease, increase a risk of disease, and affect how a person responds to medicines.

GENETIC DISEASE

Disorders Arising From Mutations in One or More Genes

Genetic diseases result from unusual nucleotide sequences in a person's genetic material. Mutations in the DNA of a cell's nucleus can lead to disease in two general ways:

- For some genetic diseases, a change in nucleotide sequences directly causes illness by affecting a protein vital for health.
- Other genetic diseases arise from a combination of factors: a change in DNA that places a person at risk for

75

a disease plus exposure to something in the environment. Disease-causing environmental factors include infection by certain viruses, exposure to certain toxic chemicals, and overexposure to the sun's ultraviolet light.

Three types of diseases are caused entirely or partly by a change in the DNA. They are single-gene disorders, multi-gene disorders, and chromosomal disorders.

Scientists have identified over 10,000 human single-gene diseases, which are caused by a mutation in one gene. In these disorders, the protein encoded by the mutated gene may be synthesized in an altered form, or the protein may not be synthesized at all. Examples of single-gene disorders include galactosemia, cystic fibrosis, and ADA deficiency.

Galactosemia: People who have this disorder lack the enzyme that converts the sugar galactose to glucose. Without the enzyme, galactose accumulates in the body, damaging the eyes, kidneys, liver, and other tissues. The most common form of the disorder results when a person inherits a mutated gene from both parents. This pattern of inheritance would have been familiar to the monk Gregor Mendel. He would have recognized that the disease has a recessive pattern of inheritance.

Cystic fibrosis: This is another genetic disease with a recessive pattern. In this case, the mutation occurs in the CFTR gene, which encodes a protein that controls the movement of salt in and out of cells. When a genetic mutation impairs the function of this protein, thick mucus builds up on the outside of cells. The mucus severely hinders breathing and digestion.

ADA deficiency: This is another recessive disorder. Here, a mutation impairs the function of the enzyme adenosine deaminase (ADA). Normally, ADA degrades a toxic chemical called deoxyadenosine. When a person lacks functional ADA enzyme, toxic chemicals accumulate in the blood and kill white blood cells, which the body relies on to fight infections of viruses and bacteria. A person who has ADA deficiency suffers repeated and severe infections, which can prove fatal.

The second type of genetic disease is the multi-gene disorder. These diseases are caused by mutations in two or more genes and may involve exposure to environmental factors. Some common disorders, such as high blood pressure, arthritis, and diabetes, are multi-gene disorders. Here are two more examples:

Retinitis pigmentosa: This disease results in a loss of vision. It is one of the simplest multi-gene disorders. A person with this disorder has mutations in two genes that encode proteins vital for vision. No environmental factors appear to be involved.

Alzheimer's disease: People who have this disorder experience a loss of brain function. The brain of an Alzheimer's patient has clusters of a mutated protein that damage brain cells. Mutations in four chromosomes have been linked to types of Alzheimer's disease. Genes in three additional chromosomes and environmental factors may also play roles in this disorder.

The third type of genetic disease is caused by a change in the structure of chromosomes. An entire chromosome, or a large part of a chromosome, can be duplicated or missing. Sometimes, the order of genes on chromosomes has changed. Down syndrome and Cri-du-Chat syndrome are two examples of chromosomal disorders.

Down syndrome: An extra copy of chromosome 21 causes this disorder. Down syndrome brings an increased risk of lung infections, digestive problems, heart defects, a loss of hearing, and some degree of mental retardation.

Cri-du-Chat syndrome: This disorder is caused by the loss of part of chromosome 5. Children with Cri-du-Chat syndrome can have breathing problems, heart defects, hearing or sight loss, and problems with their muscles.

Diseases Caused by a Variety of Mutations in Hemoglobin Genes

Packed in red blood cells, hemoglobin proteins perform a vital function in the human body. As red blood cells travel through the lungs, hemoglobins bind with oxygen molecules. As red blood cells pass by oxygen-starved tissues, hemoglobin molecules release the oxygen and pick up waste carbon dioxide molecules. During the return trip through the lungs, hemoglobins exchange carbon dioxide for oxygen. Carbon dioxide finally leaves the body in an exhaled breath.

In adults, the major form of hemoglobin has four protein subunits: two alpha-globin proteins and two beta-globin proteins. A hemoglobin molecule assembles in two steps. First, one alpha-globin protein binds with one beta-globin protein. Second, two alpha-globin/beta-globin pairs bind together to form a mature hemoglobin molecule.

Scientists have found over 400 unusual hemoglobin molecules; about half of these impair a person's health. In the following examples, a missense mutation in a beta-globin gene causes a single amino acid replacement that alters the function of hemoglobin:

- Sickle cell hemoglobin forms polymers that deform red blood cells and decrease the cells' lifespan.
- Hemoglobin C tends to crystallize in red blood cells, which shortens the life of the cells.
- Hemoglobin Hammersmith is unstable, binds oxygen weakly, and cannot deliver sufficient oxygen to tissues.
- Hemoglobin Rainer binds oxygen so tightly that less oxygen is delivered to tissues.

Some mutations decrease the amount of normal hemoglobin proteins synthesized by cells. These mutations are associated with a group of genetic diseases called the thalassemias. A decreased synthesis of alpha-globins (alpha-thalassemias) or beta-globins (beta-thalassemias) creates an imbalance in red blood cells. In alpha-thalassemia, for example, red blood cells synthesize decreased amounts of alpha-globins. This creates an excess of beta-globins, which cannot pair with alpha-globins. The extra beta-globins form clumps and damage the cell. In beta-thalassemia, excess alpha-globins clump together and harm the cell.

Many types of genetic mutations account for the thalassemias. The most common type of alpha-thalassemia results from a deletion of an alpha-globin gene. Beta-thalassemia can arise from a number of genetic alterations. These include:

- A deletion of more than 600 nucleotide bases of a beta-globin gene
- A single base replacement that decreases the rate of beta-globin gene transcription
- A single base replacement that alters RNA splicing and results in abnormal mRNA
- A single base replacement that causes beta-globin protein synthesis to end too soon
- A frameshift mutation that creates a stop codon

The most common, severe type of thalassemia in the United States is Cooley's anemia. The disease results from a complete lack of beta-globin synthesis. A person who has this disease needs frequent blood transfusions to survive.

GENE THERAPY

For more than 15 years, scientists have tried to design a new type of treatment for single-gene diseases: gene therapy. The objective of gene therapy is to correct the altered genes that are responsible for the development of disease. Depending upon the disease, researchers may want to use one of four basic tactics:

The Other Genetic Diseases: Mutations in Mitochondrial DNA

Mutations in the DNA of the cell nucleus can cause diseases or increase the risk of disease. In addition to the nucleus, other parts of the human cell also contain DNA. Mitochondria, for example, have their own DNA. Human mitochondrial DNA has about 37 genes in its 16,500 base pairs. Thirteen genes encode mitochondrial enzymes that convert products from cytoplasmic sugar breakdown into energy sources to be exported for the cell's needs. The other genes encode transfer RNA molecules and ribosomal RNA molecules.

Scientists have found over 40 diseases that are linked to changes in mitochondrial DNA. These diseases share a common feature: The genetic mutations impair the ability of mitochondria to produce energy sources. Defects in mitochondria particularly affect muscle cells and nerve cells, which require great amounts of energy to function. Hearing and vision loss, seizures, and muscle weakness are common symptoms experienced by those who have a mitochondrial disease.

- Insert into the patient's genome a transgene to encode a protein that the patient's body does not synthesize. In effect, gene therapy should enable the body to make its own medicine in the form of the missing protein.
- Regulate the extent that a mutated gene produces a mutated protein. For example, inactivating a mutated gene would help a patient if that gene encoded an altered form of a protein that harmed the patient.
- Repair a mutated gene.
- Swap a mutated gene with a copy of a normal, healthy version of the gene.

Many scientists have focused upon the first strategy, the one that is the simplest: Add a transgene that will make a protein that a patient lacks. To perform this type of gene therapy, a scientist must develop a delivery system to carry a transgene to the patient's cells. Genetically modified viruses have proved to be a popular type of delivery system. A scientist typically modifies the genetic material of a virus in at least two ways: (1) delete nucleotide sequences that contain instructions for making copies of the virus, and (2) add nucleotide sequences that encode the transgene. The genetically modified virus delivers the transgene to the cells. Once inside the cells, the virus's nucleic acid molecule inserts into the cell's chromosomes. Now, the transgene enables cells to produce the therapeutic protein.

On September 14, 1990, doctors performed the first gene therapy trial for an inherited disease, ADA deficiency. Here was a case in which the genetic cause of the disease was known (a mutation in the ADA gene), and the effect of the genetic mutation was known (lack of functional ADA enzyme). Since the disease is caused by a lack of ADA enzymes, the therapy aimed to give the patient a gene that encoded functional ADA enzyme.

At the National Institutes of Health in Maryland, doctors removed white blood cells from a four-year-old girl who had ADA deficiency. They treated her cells with genetically modified virus DNA that contained a normal ADA gene. Viral DNA containing the ADA gene was inserted into the chromosomes of the white blood cells. The doctors infused the transgenic white blood cells into their patient. During the next several years, doctors repeated the gene therapy process about a dozen times. Eventually, the patient's body

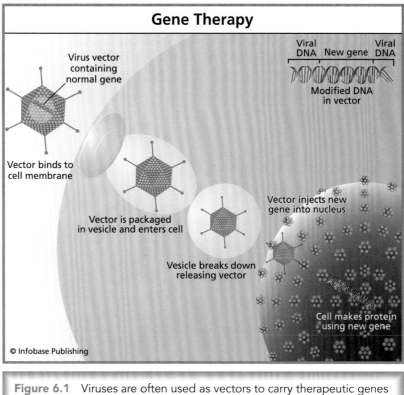

Gene Therapy

Virus vector containing normal gene

Viral DNA   New gene   Viral DNA

Modified DNA in vector

Vector binds to cell membrane

Vector is packaged in vesicle and enters cell

Vesicle breaks down releasing vector

Vector injects new gene into nucleus

Cell makes protein using new gene

© Infobase Publishing

Figure 6.1   Viruses are often used as vectors to carry therapeutic genes into host cells during gene therapy.

produced about 25% of the normal amounts of ADA enzyme. Although gene therapy did not cure the disease, the treatment improved the patient's health and helped her to experience a rather normal childhood.

These doctors used *ex vivo* gene therapy to treat ADA deficiency. In *ex vivo* gene therapy, cells are removed from a patient and are treated with DNA that contains a transgene to produce transgenic cells. The transgenic cells are then returned to the patient. A different strategy is called *in vivo* gene therapy. In this approach, a doctor administers a transgene directly to a patient.

In 2007, doctors at London's Moorfields Eye Hospital used *in vivo* gene therapy to treat a vision disorder caused by a mutation in the RPE65 gene. The mutation disrupts the function of cells in the eye's retina. To treat the disease in 12 patients, doctors inserted a

Gene Variations: Humans vs. Humans, Humans vs. Chimps

In October 1990, scientists around the globe launched the Human Genome Project. The project was a huge effort to learn the sequence of the human genome's three billion base pairs. Researchers sequenced parts of genomes of different people and collected the results. The approach was similar to constructing a puzzle with pieces gathered from different sources. When they started, scientists guessed that the project could be finished in 15 years. However, advances in DNA sequencing techniques accelerated their progress. By April 2003, scientists had sequenced a model human genome.

Early results from the project indicated that human DNA varies little from person to person. Humans share an identical order of 99.9% of their nucleotide bases. In 2007, a scientific journal presented the genome of a single person. Analysis of this genome suggests that humans are 99.0% to 99.5% identical, rather than 99.9% identical. Still, genetic similarities among humans are much greater than genetic differences.

Humans and chimpanzees, which are our closest animal relatives, share a high degree of nucleotide sequence similarity. The difference between human and chimp genomes is about 4% to 5%. The small number is deceiving, however. A difference in nucleotide sequence is just the tip of the iceberg.

Scientists propose that two groups of ancient primates separated about 5 to 7 million years ago. One group gave rise to a lineage that led to chimps and the other group gave rise to the human lineage. As the two lineages evolved, their genomes changed in important ways that did not greatly affect overall nucleotide sequences. Mutations disabled some ancient genes. Today, humans lack active genes that chimps retain and vice versa. Human cells and chimp cells also differ in the amounts of proteins synthesized. The two species further differ in the way that RNA splicing alters the amino acid sequence of proteins.

needle through the patients' eyes and into their retinas. Then, they injected virus vectors that contained copies of the normal RPE65 gene. This marked the first attempt to treat an inherited disease of the eye with gene therapy.

GENETIC VARIATION IN RESPONSE TO DRUGS

A number of genetic variations affect health by affecting how a person reacts to a drug. Many of these variations occur in genes that encode enzymes that **metabolize** drugs. An enzyme that metabolizes drugs alters the structure and properties of a drug. Metabolizing enzymes transform some drugs into inactive drugs. Enzymes can also convert an inactive medicine to an active form. Some enzymes alter a drug to make it more soluble in water to help the body excrete the drug and decrease the amount that remains in a person's bloodstream. Variations in the activity levels of drug-metabolizing enzymes determine the effectiveness of a drug and whether a person will experience toxic side effects of the drug.

The cytochrome P450 (CYP) family is a large group of enzymes that metabolize many types of drugs. Genetic variations cause differences in CYP enzyme activities, which affect how people respond to drugs. One member of the enzyme family, CYP2D6, metabolizes about 25% of all medicines. Scientists have discovered over 70 CYP2D6 gene variants. People who have low CYP2D6 enzyme activity cannot metabolize drugs at a suitable rate. Drugs can accumulate in the body with toxic results. People who have many active copies of the CYP2D6 gene can metabolize and excrete drugs very quickly. As a result, they may need higher doses of a drug to achieve a therapeutic effect.

Scientists are devising tests that reveal variations in the genes of drug-metabolizing enzymes for a patient. The long-term goal of this research is to offer "personalized medicine" where a doctor can tailor a drug treatment for an individual that ensures its effectiveness and reduces harmful side effects.

Epigenetics: Beyond the Genetic Code

WHAT IS EPIGENETICS?

In 1997, scientists in Scotland announced the birth of Dolly, the first cloned sheep. The news that scientists had made a clone—a copy of another life form—incited concerns and fears. Would clones soon replace normal farm animals? In reality, the cloned sheep turned out not to signal an age of cloning after all. Cloning of animal species has proven to be much more difficult than the general public realizes.

Suppose that a scientist wants to clone her pet mouse, named Nicky. She could try to clone the mouse by obtaining a mouse egg cell and removing the nucleus from the cell. Then, the scientist could take a skin cell from Nicky, isolate the nucleus from the skin cell, and transplant it into the egg cell. The altered egg cell would contain Nicky's entire supply of nuclear DNA. Then, the scientist could transfer the egg cell to a foster mother mouse. It might seem that the mother would give birth to a young version of Nicky. However, the egg cell may not develop into a mouse pup. And, if a mouse pup was born, it may not be identical to Nicky even though the mouse pup and Nicky would share the same nuclear DNA.

The idea of the cloning technique is simple: swap one nucleus for another nucleus. The cell with the new nucleus should develop according to instructions in the new genetic material. Yet, the success rate of cloning can be very low in many species. Hundreds of attempts may be required before a researcher obtains a surviving or viable clone. The problem is that identical DNA is not enough to guarantee success.

Two cells with identical DNA can produce different proteins due to **epigenetic** effects. Originally, the word "**epigenetics**" described something that could not be explained by genetic principles. Today, epigenetics refers to the study of changes in nuclear DNA that affect the activity of genes without changing nucleotide sequences in DNA. Cells can preserve epigenetic changes as they divide to make new cells. Some epigenetic changes can pass from a parent to offspring.

In hindsight, it is not surprising that there is something beyond the genetic code that controls gene activity. Cells in various tissues of the human body must perform different functions and produce different proteins. Even in the same tissue, gene activities vary during different stages of development. Epigenetic changes add a level of control to ensure that the correct genes are active in certain cells at the right times. One type of epigenetic fine-tuning adds a small chemical group to DNA. Another type of epigenetic tweaking alters the way that proteins wrap around the DNA molecule.

MECHANISMS OF EPIGENETICS

In 1886, Gregor Mendel published his general rules for inheritance. One rule is that genes are inherited in pairs: An offspring gets one copy of a gene from its father and one copy from its mother. Another rule is that a gene has the same function whether it came from the mother or from the father. Since Mendel's time, scientists have found that mammals have some genes that do not follow the second rule. Sometimes, it does make a difference whether a gene was inherited from the mother or from the father.

During the early 1980s, scientists discovered an epigenetic effect called **genomic imprinting**: For a small number of genes, the parental source of a gene affects gene activity. Scientists chose the term "imprinting" to signal that something inactivates a gene without changing the nucleotide sequence of the gene. An imprinted gene is inactive in the sense that transcription from the gene is turned off. Two genes encoding the same protein can be active or inactive, depending upon whether it is inherited from the father or from the mother. That is, some genes have an imprint in the set of genes inherited from the mother, while other genes have an imprint in the set of genes inherited from the father. For a particular gene, the offspring can receive an imprinted copy from either its mother or its father, but not from both.

DNA methylation, which plays a role in imprinting, is one of the best understood epigenetic changes. A methyl group is a cluster of a carbon atom and three hydrogen atoms. In DNA methylation, an enzyme attaches a methyl group to a cytosine base in a DNA molecule. Attachment of methyl groups can interfere with the cell's

Prions: The Deadly Proteins

In 1982, Stanley B. Prusiner of the University of California, San Francisco, published a bizarre proposal. He had been studying the infectious agent that causes scrapie, a central nervous system disorder that occurs in sheep. Prusiner proposed that the disease arose from an infectious protein; neither DNA nor RNA was involved in the spread of this disease. He called the infectious protein "proteinaceous infectious particle" or "**prion**." At first, many scientists called the prion idea absurd, but decades of experiments have supported Prusiner's proposal.

All mammals have prion proteins called PrPC, which stands for **Pr**ion **P**rotein-**C**ellular. These proteins can be found in brain nerve cells, where they play roles in maintaining cell function. Typical PrPC proteins have a corkscrew shape. When a PrPC protein flattens and loses its normal form, it is usually removed from the cell. The abnormal form of prion is known as PrPSc, or **Pr**ion **P**rotein-**Sc**rapie. Sometimes, cells cannot get rid of these mangled PrPSc proteins, which form large masses, harm nerve cells, machinery that synthesizes RNA from DNA. By interfering with gene transcription, methylation stops the production of the protein encoded by the gene. DNA methylation is reversible: Certain enzymes can remove methyl groups from cytosine bases.

Another type of epigenetic control involves proteins that bind with DNA. Humans have 46 chromosomes packed into the nuclei of every somatic cell. Each chromosome contains a single DNA molecule combined with **histone** proteins and nonhistone proteins. The combination of DNA and proteins is called chromatin. In chromatin, twisted, double-stranded, negatively charged DNA spools around positively charged histone proteins to create a structure that is shaped like beads on a string. Each of these "beads," which are called **nucleosomes**, consists of eight histones wrapped with a DNA segment of about 150 base pairs. DNA spacers of about 20 to

and injure the brain. A person or animal with PrPSc proteins accumulating in nerve cells shows signs of brain damage, such as a loss of muscle control. Prion diseases often lead to death.

A person can acquire PrPSc proteins due to a genetic mutation. Scientists have found over 30 types of mutations in human prion protein genes. At least three of these can cause disease: a mutation that replaces a single amino acid, a mutation that creates an early stop codon, and a mutation that adds eight-amino acid peptides into prion proteins. The mutations may produce unstable forms of PrPC that unfold into the PrPSc form.

Prion diseases also spread like typical infections. One of the best known of the animal prion disorders is mad cow disease. During the 1980s, mad cow disease affected more than two million cattle in the United Kingdom. Prusiner and his team proposed that infectious prion diseases spread because PrPSc is able to create a chain reaction. PrPSc proteins convert normal PrPC proteins into the abnormal PrPSc form. These new abnormal PrPSc proteins transform more normal PrPC proteins, and so on. In this way, the disease spreads without the need for infectious DNA or RNA.

60 base pairs separate the nucleosomes. A human chromosome has hundreds of thousands to over a million nucleosomes. The beads-on-a-string chromatin is compacted further into a dense fiber-like structure called a **solenoid**. This compacting is necessary to squeeze three billion base pairs-worth of DNA into the cell nucleus.

The structure of chromatin affects the activities of genes. A dense, compact structure blocks enzymes from gaining access to a gene for transcription. A relaxed, open structure of chromatin allows transcription to take place. Scientists have found at least nine types of chemical changes of histones. These changes in histone proteins can affect whether chromatin is compact (inactive) or loose (active).

One example of a chemical change is the addition of acetyl groups to histones. An acetyl group is a cluster of one oxygen (O) atom, two carbon (C) atoms, and three hydrogen (H) atoms. Enzymes attach an acetyl group to an amino group on a histone. An amino group has a positive electrical charge and contains a nitrogen (N) atom and three hydrogen atoms. The addition of an acetyl group $(CO-CH_3)$ to an amino group (NH_3^+) abolishes the amino group's positive charge $(NH-CO-CH_3)$. The attachment of acetyl groups neutralizes the positive charge of histones. As a result, the attraction weakens between histones and negatively-charged DNA. The weakened attraction causes the chromatin structure to unravel and allows transcription to take place. The reverse also happens. If an enzyme removes acetyl groups from histones, the proteins become more positively charged and bind more tightly to DNA. Removing acetyl groups can prevent transcription from a gene.

DNA methylation and chemical changes in histones appear to be the main types of epigenetic changes in mammals. These two epigenetic modifications are often found together. Inactive genes often occur in methylated regions of DNA with dense chromatin and histones that lack acetyl groups. Active areas of chromatin can have unmethylated DNA and large amounts of histones with acetyl groups. Patterns of DNA methylation and histone changes can be passed on when cells divide.

DNA methylation and changes in histones are vital for normal development. These epigenetic changes also play a role in the onset of diseases, especially cancer. Both histone modifications and DNA

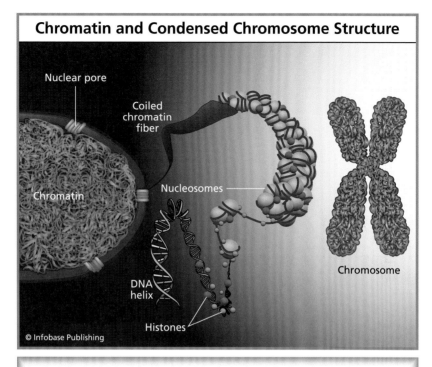

Figure 7.1 When DNA is combined with proteins, it organizes into a compact structure, a dense string-like fiber called chromatin, which condenses even further into chromosomes during cell division. Each DNA strand wraps around groups of small protein molecules called histones, forming a series of beadlike structures, called nucleosomes, connected by the DNA strand.

methylation patterns appear disturbed in tumor cells, which reproduce themselves without control. Unlike a mutation in the nucleotide sequence of a gene, an epigenetic change can be reversed. This is the basis for research into medicines that alter DNA methylation or histone chemistry. Scientists are studying drugs for possible cancer treatment that block DNA methylation enzymes and enzymes that remove acetyl groups from histones.

The Food and Drug Administration (FDA) has approved "epigenetic drugs" for the treatment of myelodysplastic syndromes. People who have these disorders cannot produce normal amounts of healthy blood cells. The drugs azacitidine (trademarked Vidaza) and

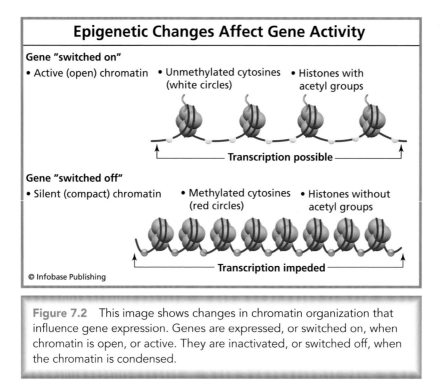

Epigenetic Changes Affect Gene Activity

Gene "switched on"
- Active (open) chromatin
- Unmethylated cytosines (white circles)
- Histones with acetyl groups

Transcription possible

Gene "switched off"
- Silent (compact) chromatin
- Methylated cytosines (red circles)
- Histones without acetyl groups

Transcription impeded

© Infobase Publishing

Figure 7.2   This image shows changes in chromatin organization that influence gene expression. Genes are expressed, or switched on, when chromatin is open, or active. They are inactivated, or switched off, when the chromatin is condensed.

decitabine (trademarked Dacogen) decrease DNA methylation and are thought to reverse abnormal DNA methylation patterns. These drug treatments stimulate immature blood cells to develop into mature blood cells.

RNA CAN INTERFERE WITH ACTIVE GENES

Around 1990, scientists began to discover a new way that cells fine-tune gene activity. A clue to this was found during efforts to alter the color of petunias. At DNA Plant Technology Corporation (located in Oakland, California), Richard Jorgenson and his team made transgenic petunias, in which the transgene encoded the enzyme chalcone synthase. They designed the transgene to produce large amounts of chalcone synthase mRNA. Since the enzyme is needed for the biosynthesis of pigments responsible for purple coloration,

Using RNA Interference to Treat Diseases

In some genetic diseases, a mutation causes cells to produce either an abnormal form of a protein or too much of a normal protein. These diseases may be treated by either shutting off the synthesis of the abnormal protein or by reducing the excess synthesis of a normal protein. In viral infections, a virus's nucleic acid molecule takes control of a cell, forcing cellular machinery to produce proteins for new viruses. The spread of viruses from cell to cell can be stopped by blocking the synthesis of viral proteins. Scientists have been searching for ways to take advantage of RNAi in the treatment of diseases. RNAi would target selected mRNAs for destruction and shut off the synthesis of proteins encoded by the target mRNAs.

One of the companies working on RNAi therapies is Alnylam Pharmaceuticals (located in Cambridge, Massachusetts). Alnylam scientists produce double-stranded RNA molecules that have a length of about 23 base pairs. These "small interfering RNAs" (siRNAs) are designed to have nucleotide sequences that match part of the nucleotide sequence in a target mRNA molecule. After siRNA enters a cell, it unwinds and combines with RISC, the multiprotein complex. When siRNA-RISC encounters a target mRNA, the mRNA attaches to the siRNA by base pairing. This proves fatal to the mRNA, which is cleaved and then degraded. The siRNA-RISC moves on to destroy more target mRNAs.

Alnylam researchers are designing RNAi therapies for various diseases, including liver cancer. One of their RNAi therapies shuts off the synthesis of two proteins that promote the growth of tumors. In 2007, the company reported successful results from early studies in laboratory animals. Alnylam scientists have also been developing an RNAi treatment for respiratory syncytial virus (RSV) infections.

(continues)

(continued)

RSV is a very contagious virus that infects the lungs. Re-searchers designed a siRNA that stops the production of RSV viruses. In an infected cell, the siRNA destroys mRNA that encodes a viral protein needed for reproduction of the virus. This stops the virus from invading other lung cells. Al-nylam started tests of the RNAi therapy in human patients during 2007.

the scientists expected the transgenic petunias would have flowers with a deep purple color. Yet, some of the plants had white flowers that lacked purple coloration. By giving plant cells extra copies of the chalcone synthase gene, they had somehow inactivated the synthesis of purple pigment. Soon, other researchers reported this strange gene-silencing effect in various types of transgenic plants.

Years later, Andrew Fire, who was at the Carnegie Institution of Washington at that time, found another clue while studying roundworms. Fire and his group injected double-stranded RNA into roundworms. The RNA stopped the production of protein encoded by any gene with the same nucleotide sequence as the injected RNA. They named the gene silencing effect **RNA interference**, or RNAi.

Fire and his team reported their experiments in 1998. Three years later, other groups reported the RNAi effect in human cells. Today, scientists view RNAi as a natural process in animal cells, plant cells, and fungal cells. RNAi regulates the activity of many genes and controls the development of embryos.

One RNAi pathway starts with the synthesis of RNA molecules that have nucleotide sequences identical to parts of a gene. Enzymes cut the RNA molecules into pieces about 22 nucleotides long. Not surprisingly, the tiny RNA molecules are called **micro-RNAs**. Scientists propose that the cells of plants, fungi, and animals produce thousands or tens of thousands of different micro-RNAs. These micro-RNAs may play a role in controlling at least 70% of a cell's protein-encoding genes.

Micro-RNAs can inhibit the synthesis of a protein in two ways. In both cases, a micro-RNA binds to a multi-protein structure called the "RNA-induced silencing complex," or RISC. When it finds its target mRNA, micro-RNA-RISC attaches to the mRNA by base pairing with the micro-RNA. Burdened with its micro-RNA-RISC passenger, the mRNA gamely loads onto ribosomes for translation. However, the presence of one or more micro-RNA-RISC bundles clinging to the mRNA blocks ribosome movement and stops protein synthesis.

Micro-RNAs can also inhibit protein synthesis by destroying mRNA before it can reach ribosomes. In this process, micro-RNA-RISC attaches to the mRNA by base pairing, and then RISC cleaves the target mRNA. Then, as enzymes rapidly degrade the cleaved mRNA to bits, micro-RNA-RISC seeks its next mRNA target.

RNA interference complements the two epigenetic processes described above. Epigenetic changes activate or inactivate genes at the source by enabling or blocking transcription. After transcription, RNA interference controls protein synthesis by blocking translation or by destroying mRNA. All of these processes allow cells to fine-tune the expression of genes.

Scientific Challenges and Ethical Disputes

I n 1961, Marshall Nirenberg and Heinrich Matthaei showed that the sequence UUU found in mRNA caused the addition of the amino acid phenylalanine to a protein. They had discovered the first word of the genetic code. Since its discovery, the genetic code has inspired many debates. Scientists and the public have argued about how—or if—the code should be used to alter life forms.

TRANSGENIC PLANTS: FRANKENFOODS AND RUNAWAY GENES

In the December 24, 1961, issue of the *New York Herald Tribune*, science reporter Earl Ubell wondered what scientists would do next once they had cracked the genetic code. "If biologists know the whole hereditary code and learn how to change it at will," he wrote, "they may be able to control heredity by chemical means. They could raise plants and animals of almost any desired character, and do it in a hurry."

Although scientists cannot yet produce a transgenic plant "in a hurry," the farming of genetically engineered plants has become routine. In a December 2007 essay, FDA attorney Mark Schwartz wrote that U.S. farmers have widely adopted genetic technology, stating that 90% of soybeans, about 80% of cotton, and 60% of corn planted in 2007 had been genetically modified. "Fully three-quarters of the processed foods in American supermarkets," Schwartz continued, "contain ingredients from recombinant DNA modified plants." In the United States, he said, "dozens of new crops and foods resulting from recombinant DNA technology have been marketed over the past decade, and they have been an overwhelming success." This is not to say that people who live outside the United States, or even everybody who lives within this country, have embraced the practice of altering crop genes.

U.S. farmers planted the first large-scale transgenic crops in 1996. This event sparked a lasting dispute about the wisdom of genetically modified (GM) food. The following headlines reflect how intense and wide-ranging this debate is:

- "Trade War Threat Over Genetically Altered Soya." Charles Arthur. *The Independent* (London, England), September 30, 1996.
- "Genetic Soybeans Alarm Europeans." Youssef M. Ibrahim. *The New York Times*, November 7, 1996.
- "Do GM Crops Pose a Threat?" Jeff Rooker. *The News Letter* (Belfast, Northern Ireland), May 22, 1999.
- "Vatican Theologians Say 'Prudent Yes' to GM foods." Antony Barnett. *The Observer* (United Kingdom), November 28, 1999.
- "Gene-altered Corn Changes Dynamics of Grain Industry." David Barboza. *The New York Times*, December 11, 2000.
- "Food Groups Seek Moratorium on Pharma Crops." Neil Franz. *Chemical Week*, February 19, 2003.
- "Trans-Atlantic Food Fight: The Stakes in the U.S.-Europe Battle Over Genetically Engineered Crops." John Feffer. *The American Prospect*, May 2003.
- "Top GM Food Company Abandons British Crop Trials." Robin McKie. *The Observer* (United Kingdom), September 28, 2003.
- "Will Frankenfood Save the Planet?" Jonathan Rauch. *The Atlantic Monthly*, October 2003.

- "Gene-altered Crops Denounced." Rick Weiss. *The Washington Post*, August 16, 2006.
- "Ah-tchoo! Do Genetically Modified Foods Cause Allergies?" Starre Vartan. *E*, November 2006.
- "Proceed with Caution Over Genetically Modified Crops." Paddy Rooney. *Western Mail* (Cardiff, Wales), November 16, 2004.
- "Human Genes in Your Food? Rice Crops To Be Genetically Modified with Human DNA." Sean Poulter. *Daily Mail* (London, England), March 6, 2007.
- "Judge Stops Sale of Monsanto's Genetically Engineered Alfalfa." Andrew Pollack. *The New York Times*, March 13, 2007.
- "Thailand: Green Groups Seek Court Ruling Against GM Crops." Marwaan Macan-Markar. *Inter Press Service English News Wire*, January 9, 2008.

Those who oppose transgenic crops highlight possible risks to human health and the environment. One argument against transgenic crops is that altering genes might accidentally enable a plant to produce a molecule toxic to humans. Another argument is that cultivating transgenic plants that make insecticidal proteins could harm the environment by killing insects that do not feed on crops. The death of these non-target insects would affect birds, fish and other animals that eat the insects. Scientists around the world study the use of transgenic crop technology for any ill effects.

ALTERING AND ANALYZING HUMAN GENES

In his 1961 *New York Herald Tribune* article, Earl Ubell wrote that knowledge of the genetic code could lead to treatments for human hereditary diseases. At the same time, a genetic technology "could be applied to control the intelligence of large human populations wholesale [and] breed a super-race."

The possibility of altering a human's DNA also concerned Marshall Nirenberg. In 1967, *Science* published an essay he wrote that offered a warning: One day, people may be able to shape their own biologic destiny by altering their DNA. The article states:

[M]an may be able to program his own cells with synthetic information long before he will be able to assess adequately the long-term consequences of such alterations, long before he will be able to formulate goals, and long before he can resolve the ethical and moral problems which will be raised. When man becomes capable of instructing his own cells, he must refrain from doing so until he has sufficient wisdom to use this knowledge for the benefit of mankind.

Genetically Engineered Taco Shells

A type of transgenic corn called StarLink produces Cry9c, a protein that kills certain insects. Scientists added a Cry9c gene into the corn's genome to protect the plant from the cornstalk borer, the corn earworm, and other insect pests. In 1998, the U.S. Environmental Protection Agency (EPA) approved StarLink corn for use in animal feed and for non-food industrial uses, such as the production of alcohol. The EPA did not approve StarLink corn for use in human food. At the time, EPA scientists were concerned that Cry9c protein could produce a slightly toxic effect in humans.

In September 2000, researchers detected StarLink corn residues in some taco shells. The transgenic corn had entered the human food supply. By accident, a small amount of StarLink corn had mixed with a large amount of natural corn. Companies recalled nearly 300 corn-based products. Over 70 types of corn chips were removed from grocery store shelves. Corn shipments destined for human food use had to be diverted to the two permitted uses of StarLink corn.

In time, concerns about toxic taco shells and corn chips were put to rest. In June 2001, the Centers for Disease Control and Prevention reported that its scientists had failed to uncover any evidence of toxicity. In October 2007, the EPA announced the results of over four million tests on four billion bushels of corn. The tests had not detected traces of Cry9c in the human food supply for at least three years.

Today, scientists and doctors alter the genetic instructions of human cells. Current gene therapy is designed to treat a disorder in a specific individual. An ongoing debate focuses on whether these techniques should be used to genetically alter the human species. Another dispute concerns the detection of inherited diseases of individuals and the use of this genetic information.

Gene Therapy Controversies

In theory, a genetic disease may be treated by two types of gene therapy: **germline** genetic modification and somatic gene therapy. Germline genetic modification could be used to add a nucleotide sequence to a person's egg cells or sperm cells to alter future generations. This technique could change more than disease-related genes. Attempts might be made to "upgrade" intelligence, athletic performance, and other traits. As Ubell warned, humans might be tempted to breed a super-race. Religious leaders and others have argued for a ban on a technology that could lead to designer babies with better-than-normal traits. So far, germline genetic modification of humans has remained a theory; no one has reported an attempt of this technique.

The aim of somatic gene therapy is to treat a person who has an inherited disorder by adding or changing a nucleotide sequence in the DNA of somatic cells. Doctors performed the first somatic gene therapy test for an inherited disease in 1990—the treatment of a young girl who had ADA deficiency. The doctors modified their patient's white blood cells by inserting a normal ADA gene into the chromosomes.

The ADA deficiency treatment inspired researchers around the world to perform clinical trials for treating a variety of disorders. After ten years of attempts, scientists reported few successes. Worse yet, news about tragic failures in this area surfaced. In 1999, a patient died during a gene therapy trial in Pennsylvania. This tragedy appears to have marked the first time that gene therapy caused a death. In 2003, two children developed cancer during a gene therapy trial that was conducted in France.

Clinical trials have revealed unforeseen barriers to gene therapy. In many clinical trials, researchers added a transgene to human cells with a vector that was produced from altered virus nucleic acid. As it turns out, when these viruses deliver a transgene to human DNA, the transgene inserts in a random place in a chromosome. A random insertion can activate a gene that harms the patient. The two children in the gene therapy trial in France, for example, appear to have developed cancer because viral DNA had inserted in a way that promoted the growth of cancer cells.

Epigenetic changes play a role in the success of gene therapy. DNA methylation and the removal of acetyl groups from histones can inactivate a therapeutic transgene. RNA interference may also limit the effect of a gene therapy by decreasing the production of the protein encoded by a transgene. According to the *Journal of Gene Medicine*, about 700 gene therapy clinical trials were approved worldwide from 2000 to mid-2007. These studies with patients should reveal the safety and value of many types of treatments. As scientists learn more about epigenetic effects and RNA interference, they can design ways to overcome current limitations of gene therapy.

Genetic Testing: What's in Your Genome?

Three types of genetic tests can reveal whether a person has an inherited disease. Analysis of a tissue sample may show that a person lacks an enzyme or a protein associated with a disorder. A microscopic study of cells can show whether a person has altered chromosomes. Alternatively, DNA can be isolated from a tissue sample and analyzed for the presence of a mutated gene.

Laboratories now perform over 1,000 genetic tests for a wide range of diseases. These tests are carried out for various reasons, including:

- *Newborn screening.* All states in the United States require the genetic testing of healthy-appearing newborns. Every year, labs test blood samples taken from millions of infants. One of the tests can detect a disorder called **phenylketonuria**. An infant who is found to have this disorder can be put on a restricted diet to prevent the development of mental retardation.
- *Carrier testing.* Individuals may request a genetic test to determine whether they are a carrier for a recessive disease.

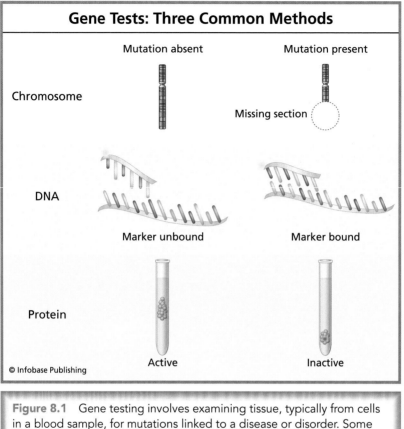

Gene Tests: Three Common Methods

Mutation absent

Mutation present

Chromosome

Missing section

DNA

Marker unbound

Marker bound

Protein

Active

Inactive

© Infobase Publishing

Figure 8.1   Gene testing involves examining tissue, typically from cells in a blood sample, for mutations linked to a disease or disorder. Some tests identify changes in whole chromosomes. Others examine short sections of DNA with genes, or look for the protein products of genes.

In genetic medicine, a carrier is an individual who has inherited one copy of a disease gene from either the mother or father. If two people who are carriers have a child, then their child may inherit a copy of the disease gene from both parents. If so, then the child will have the disease.

• *Prenatal testing.* Carrier testing or family histories may indicate that a couple has a high risk of having a child with a certain genetic disease. If so, then the couple may request a test of their fetus to detect the disease. Individuals of advanced age may also want prenatal testing. In North America, pregnant women who are older than 35 years often request an analysis of fetal chromosomes in order to detect Down's syndrome and other disorders.

- *Predictive testing.* This type of genetic test can reveal whether a currently healthy person is at risk to develop a disease in the future. A positive test for some diseases can lead to treatment that prevents the disease. However, some inherited diseases that develop late in life have no treatment. Genetic counselors offer advice for people who are deciding whether or not to take a test to detect an untreatable disease.

- *Testing for genetic risk factors.* These tests identify a person's risk for developing a common and complex disease, such as cancer, diabetes, or heart disease. In these cases, genes do not *determine* that a particular individual will develop a certain disease, but rather, the genes make that person *more susceptible* to developing a disease. Doctors can use data about genetic risk factors to help their patients maintain good health.

Genetic testing has sparked a number of debates, especially in the area of prenatal testing. A prenatal diagnosis may reveal that the fetus has an untreatable and devastating genetic disease. If so, the diagnosis may lead to a decision to end the pregnancy. Such a decision offends those who absolutely oppose abortion. Even more controversial is a decision to end pregnancy if a fetus has a treatable disease, a disorder that causes a mild cosmetic defect, or if a fetus, in the parents' view, has the wrong gender. In time, scientists will identify genes associated with high intelligence and popular physical traits. Should parents use prenatal testing to screen for their perfect child? Would this be another way to breed a super race?

A general dispute in the area of genetic testing focuses on the use of an individual person's genetic data. An employer may want access to such information in order to hire employees who have a low risk of developing a disease. Health insurance companies and life insurance companies would also benefit from accessing genetic information before agreeing to insure a person. In the United States, Congress and state legislators have been enacting laws to protect a person's genetic data. Laws also ban an employer or health insurance company from discriminating against people on the basis of genetic test information.

THERE IS STILL MUCH TO DO

In 1865, Gregor Mendel published his studies on the inheritance of traits in pea plants. He devised rules that required the existence of "units of inheritance," which later became known as genes. By 1966, scientists had learned that genes reside in chromosomes, that they direct the synthesis of proteins, and that a genetic code enables cells to use data stored in the DNA double helix to synthesize messenger RNA and protein. The invention of rapid DNA sequencing techniques during the 1970s and 1980s enabled the Human Genome Project of 1990. The massive effort produced its share of surprising results:

Cleaning the Environment with Transgenic Plants

Critics of transgenic plant technology argue that the plants will pollute nature. At the same time, scientists are using transgenic know-how to create plants that will clean up the environment. Neil C. Bruce of the University of York, United Kingdom, led a research team who inserted a bacterial enzyme gene into tobacco plant cells. Bacteria that have this particular enzyme can degrade the explosive TNT, which pollutes the ground of military training ranges and TNT manufacturing facilities, into nontoxic chemicals. By using the bacterial enzyme, the transgenic tobacco plants detoxified TNT-contaminated soil.

Sharon Doty and her colleagues at the University of Washington, Seattle, produced transgenic poplar tree plants capable of removing a toxic compound from groundwater. These plants have a rabbit gene that encodes an enzyme found in liver cells. In lab tests, pieces of genetically altered poplar plants extracted 91% of the chemical from a toxin-laced solution. Normal popular plants removed a mere 3%. Thanks to a boosted supply of enzymes, the transgenic plants degraded the toxic substance 100 times faster than normal plants. The transgenic poplars also extracted two types of chemical poisons from the air.

- Humans have about 20,000 protein-encoding genes, many fewer than predictions of 80,000 to 140,000 genes.
- Human chromosomes have pockets of gene-dense nucleotide sequences surrounded by large, gene-poor regions.
- Less than 2% of the human genome encodes proteins.

The discovery that a very small fraction of human DNA encodes proteins raised a question: What is the function of the majority of human DNA? Following the Human Genome Project, scientists found that many regions of DNA produce RNA molecules that do not encode proteins. Some scientists refer to these areas of DNA as transcribed fragments, or "transfrags." Others propose to change the definition of gene to include these DNA regions. At one time, a gene was viewed as a DNA nucleotide sequence that encodes a protein. Today, scientists consider a gene to be a DNA nucleotide sequence that encodes a functional product. The product can be a protein, an RNA molecule with a known function, such as tRNA, or an RNA molecule with a function that is yet to be determined.

While many researchers sequenced the human genome, other researchers showed that the genetic code alone does not control protein synthesis. Epigenetic changes—DNA methylation and chromatin structure—also manage gene activity. RNA interference added another type of control over the synthesis of proteins.

In his autobiography, *What Mad Pursuit* (1988), Francis Crick reveals how he decided to become a scientist as a young child:

> But I foresaw one snag. By the time I grew up—and how far away that seemed!—everything would have been discovered. I confided my fears to my mother, who reassured me. "Don't worry, Ducky," she said. "There will be plenty left for you to find out."

Mrs. Crick's forecast remains true. Studies of the human genome prove that much remains to be discovered.

Glossary

amino acid   The chemical building block of a protein

anticodon   A sequence of three nucleotides on transfer-RNA that can form base pairs with a codon on messenger-RNA

axon   A long, thin extension of a nerve cell that transfers electrical signals from the cell body

bacteriophage   A virus that infects bacteria

base   A molecule that forms part of DNA and RNA

base pair   Two bases from two nucleotides, held together by weak bonds, in a double-stranded DNA or RNA molecule

biolistics   A method for introducing foreign DNA into cells by bombarding the cells with DNA-coated microprojectiles

black light   A lamp that radiates invisible ultraviolet light

chemical bond   A link created when two atoms of different chemicals share electrons

chromatin   A mixture of proteins, DNA, and RNA

chromosome   A structure in a cell that contains DNA

codon   A group of three nucleotides; most codons code for an amino acid

codon bias   Different preferences among different organisms for one or more codons that encode a particular amino acid

culture   Biological material grown under controlled conditions

cytoplasm   The organized complex of fluid and organelles outside the nuclear membrane of a cell

cytoskeleton   The network of long proteins that control cell shape and cause movement

cytosol   The fluid material outside the nucleus and the organelles

deoxyribonuclease   An enzyme that digests DNA molecules

deoxyribonucleic acid (DNA)   A nucleic acid molecule that encodes genetic information and contains deoxyribose sugar

deoxyribose   A five-carbon sugar called ribose that is missing an oxygen atom (deoxy-) on its second carbon; a part of a nucleotide which makes up DNA molecules

dominant trait   A trait expressed by offspring even though only one parent expresses the trait

endoplasmic reticulum   A system of membranes in the cytoplasm and a site of protein synthesis

enzyme   A protein that increases the rate of a chemical reaction

epigenetic   Changes in a gene's function that do not involve changing nucleotide sequences in DNA

epigenetics   Study of changes in DNA that affect the activity of genes without changing nucleotide sequences in DNA

eukaryotic   A cell that contains a nucleus, or an organism with cells that contain nuclei

ex vivo   Experimentation performed on living cells or tissues after removal from an organism

exon   Nucleotide sequences that occur in DNA and in pre-mRNA transcripts that encode portions of a protein; exons of a pre-mRNA transcript are spliced together to form the final nucleotide sequence of mRNA for translation into protein.

fluorescent   The emission of light immediately after the absorption of light at a different wavelength

frameshift mutation   The insertion or deletion of a nucleotide in DNA that changes the reading frame of a nucleotide sequence that encodes protein

gamete   An egg cell or a sperm cell

gene   A nucleotide sequence that encodes a protein or a functional RNA molecule, such as tRNA

gene therapy   A treatment of a genetic disorder that aims to replace or to supplement an abnormal gene with a normal gene

genetic code   The collection of 64 codons that specify 20 amino acids and the signals for stopping protein synthesis

genome   The complete nucleotide sequences of an individual or species

genomic imprinting   An epigenetic effect in which the parental source of a gene affects gene activity

germline   The cells from which gametes develop

Golgi bodies   Also called Golgi apparatus; disk-shaped cytoplasmic organelles that transport protein

hemoglobin   The protein in red blood cells that carries oxygen; composed of four subunits

herbicide   A chemical used to kill plants or to reduce plant growth

histone   Protein associated with DNA in chromatin

hydrophilic   To have an affinity for water

hydrophobic   To lack an affinity for water and have a tendency to repel water

in vivo   An experiment or procedure performed in the living body of an organism

insecticide   A chemical used to kill insects

intron   Nucleotide sequences that occur in DNA and in pre-mRNA transcripts and that do not encode portions of a protein; to form mRNA for translation into protein, introns of a pre-mRNA transcripts are cut out and exons are spliced together

ligase   An enzyme that promotes the binding of two DNA fragments

lysosome   A cellular organelle that contains enzymes that break down complex chemicals for reuse by the cell

meiosis   A type of cell division required to produce egg cells and sperm cells

messenger RNA (mRNA)   An RNA molecule that transmits genetic information from DNA to a cell's protein-making apparatus

metabolize   To alter a molecule

micro-RNAs Short RNA molecules that play a role in controlling protein-encoding genes

missense mutation A DNA alteration that changes a codon to code for a different amino acid

mitochondria Organelles that function as a cell's power plant

mitosis A type of cell division that produces two identical daughter cells

mutation A change in the nucleotide sequence of a DNA molecule or a change in the amino acid sequence of a protein

nonsense mutation Mutation that creates a stop codon from a codon that encoded an amino acid

nuclear envelope A membrane that separates the contents of the nucleus from the cytoplasm

nucleic acid Any nucleotide chain(s) of DNA or RNA

nuclein A substance isolated from cell nuclei that contains DNA

nucleosome Globular subunits of chromatin composed of DNA and histones

nucleotide The monomer of DNA which contains a sugar molecule, a chemical group that contains phosphorus, and a base

nucleus The organelle that contains most of a cell's DNA

organelle A membrane-bound structure that performs a function within a cell

peptide A short chain of linked amino acids

phage A bacteriophage

phenylketonuria An inherited disorder of metabolism in which an enzyme is missing for the break down of the amino acid phenylalanine, resulting in accumulations of phenylalanine which can cause mental retardation and seizures; can be controlled by diet

plasmid Extrachromosomal rings of DNA found mostly in bacteria and capable of independent replication

point mutation A substitution of a single nucleotide for another nucleotide in a DNA sequence

polymer A large chemical made by combining smaller chemical units

primary structure   Sequence of amino acids in a protein

prion   An infectious protein

prokaryotic   A single-celled organism that lacks a nucleus

pronucleus   An egg cell nucleus or a sperm cell nucleus found in an egg cell after fusion with a sperm cell

protease   An enzyme that digests proteins

protein   A polymer of amino acids

quaternary structure   Complex of two or more similar or dissimilar protein subunits that form an active molecule

reading frame   Grouping of nucleotides into triplets that may encode a protein

recessive trait   A trait that may be expressed in offspring if both parents carry a gene for the recessive trait.

recombinant DNA   DNA that has been altered in the lab by the addition or deletion of nucleotide sequences

restriction enzyme   A protein that cleaves a DNA molecule at or near a certain nucleotide sequence

ribonuclease (RNase)   An enzyme that digests RNA

ribonucleic acid (RNA)   A nucleic acid molecule that can encode genetic information and contains ribose sugar

ribose   A five-carbon sugar that forms part of a nucleotide that makes up RNA molecules

ribosome   Structure within a cell that contains proteins and RNA and enables the translation of mRNA

RNA interference (RNAi)   A process that decreases or blocks protein synthesis

secondary structure   Helical or sheetlike structures formed by hydrogen bonding within a protein chain

silent mutation   A DNA alteration that does not result in a change in the amino acid sequence of a protein

solenoid   A dense, coiled structure of chromatin

somatic cell   A cell other than an egg cell or a sperm cell

tertiary structure   Three-dimensional shape of a protein formed by the arrangement of secondary structures

therapeutic   For use in the treatment of a disease or disorder

totipotent   The ability of a cell to develop into a whole organism or into cells of any of its tissues

transcription   The process of making an RNA copy of a DNA nucleotide sequence

transfer RNA (tRNA)   An RNA molecule that enables protein synthesis by binding to mRNA and an amino acid

transformation   The alteration of the genetics of a cell by introduction of foreign DNA

transgene   A gene that is transferred to a cell, for example, in gene therapy

transgenic   Describes an organism that has been genetically altered using recombinant DNA technology

translation   The process of making a protein using genetic code information in messenger RNA

vector   In biotechnology, a DNA molecule that can be used to deliver a transgene

wobble   The ability of a tRNA molecule to bind with more than one type of base triplet in mRNA that encodes the same amino acid

Bibliography

Abid, K. and C. Soto. "The Intriguing Prion Disorders." *Cellular and Molecular Life Sciences* 63 (2006): 2342–2351.

"Agricultural Biotechnology: Benefits Delivered," Biotechnology Industry Organization Web Site. Available online. URL: http://www.bio.org.

Al-Babili, Salim and Peter Beyer. "Golden Rice—Five Years on the Road—Five Years to Go?" *Trends in Plant Science* 10 (2005): 565–573.

Allis, C. David, Thomas Jenuwein, Danny Reinberg, and Marie-Laure Caparros, eds. *Epigenetics.* Woodbury, New York: Cold Spring Harbor Press, 2007.

Ambrogelly, Alexandre, Sotiria Palioura, and Dieter Söll. "Natural Expansion of the Genetic Code." *Nature Chemical Biology* 3 (2007): 29–35.

Arthur, Charles. "Trade War Threat over Genetically Altered Soya." *The Independent* (London), September 30, 1996.

Baruch, Susannah. "Human Germline Genetic Modification: Issues and Options for Policymakers," Genetics & Public Policy Center Web Site. Available online. URL: http://www.DNApolicy.org.

Bernstein, Bradley E., Alexander Meissner, and Eric S. Lander. "The Mammalian Epigenome." *Cell* 128 (2007): 669–681.

Bestor, Timothy H. "Gene Silencing as a Threat to the Success of Gene Therapy." *Journal of Clinical Investigation* 105 (2000): 409–411.

Brault, Aaron C., Claire Y-H Huang, Stanley A. Langevin, Richard M. Kinney, Richard A. Bowen, Wanichaya N. Ramey, Nicholas A. Panella et al. "A Single Positively Selected West Nile Viral Mutation Confers Increased Virogenesis in American Crows." *Nature Genetics* 39 (2007): 1162–1166.

"*Burkholderia mallei* Causes Glanders and Was Used as a Biological Weapon in the American Civil War and Both World Wars." European Bioinformatics Web Site. Available online. URL: http://www.ebi.ac.uk/2can/genomes/bacteria/Burkholderia_mallei.html.

Cabral, Ana Lucia B., Kil S. Lee, and Vilma R. Martins. "Regulation of the Cellular Prion Protein Gene Expression Depends on Chromatin Conformation." *Journal of Biological Chemistry* 277 (2002): 5675–5682.

Casey, Denise. "Primer on Molecular Genetics," Human Genome Project Site. Available online. URL: http://www.ornl.gov/sci/techresources/Human_Genome/publicat/primer/toc.html.

Choi, Charles Q. "Old MacDonald's Pharm." *Scientific American* 295 (September 2006): 24.

Clamp, Michele, Ben Fry, Mike Kamal, Xiaohui Xie, James Cuff, Michael F. Lin, Manolis Kellis et al. "Distinguishing Protein-coding and Noncoding Genes in the Human Genome." *Proceedings of the National Academy of Science, USA* 104 (2007): 19428–19433.

Collinge, John and Anthony R. Clarke. "A General Model of Prion Strains and Their Pathogenicity." *Science* 318 (2007): 930–936.

Committee on Genetically Modified Pest-Protected Plants, National Research Council. *Genetically Modified Pest-Protected Plants: Science and Regulation.* Washington, D.C.: The National Academies Press, 2000.

Crick, F.H.C., Leslie Barnett, S. Brenner, and R.J. Watts-Tobin. "General Nature of the Genetic Code for Proteins." *Nature* 192 (1961): 1227–1232.

Crick, Francis. *What Mad Pursuit: A Personal View of Scientific Discovery.* New York: Basic Books, 1988.

Crommelin, Daan J.A. and Robert D. Sindelar, eds. *Pharmaceutical Biotechnology.* London: Harwood Academic Publishers, 1997.

Dahm, Ralf. "Friedrich Miescher and the Discovery of DNA." *Developmental Biology* 278 (2005): 274–288.

de Fougerolles, Antonin, Hans-Peter Vornlocher, John Maraganore, and Judy Lieberman. "Interfering with Disease: A Progress Report on siRNA-based Therapeutics." *Nature Reviews Drug Discovery* 6 (2007): 443–453.

Devlin, Thomas M., ed. *Textbook of Biochemistry with Clinical Correlations,* 4th ed. New York: Wiley-Liss, Inc., 1997.

Doty, Sharon L., C. Andrew James, Allison L. Moore, Azra Vajzovic, Glenda L. Singleton, Caiping Ma, Zareen Khan et al. "Enhanced Phytoremediation of Volatile Environmental Pollutants with Transgenic Trees." *Proceedings of the National Academy of Sciences, USA* 104 (2007): 16816–16821.

Downward, Julian. "RNA Interference." *British Medical Journal* 328 (2004): 1245–1248.

Eapen, Susan, Sudhir Singh, and S.F. D'Souza. "Advances in Development of Transgenic Plants for Remediation of Xenobiotic Pollutants." *Biotechnology Advances* 25 (2007): 442–451.

"EPA Draft White Paper Regarding StarLink® Corn Dietary Exposure and Risk; Availability for Comment." *Federal Register* 72 (2007): 58978–58980.

Feinberg, Andrew P. "Phenotypic Plasticity and the Epigenetics of Human Disease." *Nature* 447 (2007): 433–440.

Francks, C., S. Maegawa, J. Laurén, B.S. Abrahams, A. Velayos-Baeza, S.E. Medland, S. Colella et al. "LRRTM1 on Chromosome 2p12 is a Maternally Suppressed Gene That is Associated Paternally with Handedness and Schizophrenia." *Molecular Psychiatry* 12 (2007): 1129–1139.

Freeland Stephen J. and Laurence D. Hurst. "Evolution Encoded." *Scientific American* 290 (April 2004): 84–91.

"Gene Testing," Human Genome Project Information Web Site. Available online. URL: http://web.ornl.gov/sci/techresources/Human_Genome/medicine/genetest.shtml.

Gerstein, Mark B., Can Bruce, Joel S. Rozowsky, Deyou Zheng, Jiang Du, Jan O. Korbel, Olof Emanuelsson et al. "What is a Gene, Post-ENCODE? History and Updated Definition." *Genome Research* 17 (2007): 669–681.

Ghosh, Pallab. "Gene Therapy First for Poor Sight," BBC News Web Site. Available online. URL: http://news.bbc.co.uk.

Glick, Bernard R. and Jack J. Pasternak. *Molecular Biotechnology*, 3rd ed. Washington, D.C.: ASM Press, 2003.

Goldberg, Aaron D., C. David Allis, and Emily Bernstein. "Epigenetics: A Landscape Takes Shape." *Cell* 128 (2007): 635–638.

"Golden Rice: Sustainable Biofortification for the Poor Rural Population," Golden Rice Project Web Site. Available online. URL: http://www.goldenrice.org.

Griffiths, Anthony J.F., Susan R. Wessler, Richard C. Lewontin, and Sean B. Carroll. *Introduction to Genetic Analysis*, 9th ed. New York: W.H. Freeman and Company, 2008.

Gu, S., D.A. Thompson, C.R. Srikumari, B. Lorenz, U. Finckh, A. Nicoletti, K.R. Murthy et al. "Mutations in RPE65 Cause Autosomal Recessive Childhood-onset Severe Retinal Dystrophy." *Nature Genetics* 17 (1997): 194–197.

Harris, Henry. *The Birth of the Cell.* New Haven, Conn.: Yale University Press, 1999.

Hartwell, Leland H., Leroy Hood, Michael L. Goldberg, Ann E. Reynolds, Lee M. Silver, and Ruth C. Veres. *Genetics: From Genes to Genomes*, 3rd ed. New York: McGraw-Hill, 2008.

Hayes, Brian. "The Invention of the Genetic Code." *American Scientist* 86 (January–February 1998): 8–14.

Haygood, Ralph, Oliver Fedrigo, Brian Hanson, Ken-Daigoro Yokoyama, and Gregory A. Wray. "Promoter Regions of Many Neural- and Nutri-tion-related Genes Have Experienced Positive Selection During Human Evolution." *Nature Genetics* 39 (2007): 1140–1144.

Henikoff, Steven. "Nucleosome Destabilization in the Epigenetic Regula-tion of Gene Expression." *Nature Reviews Genetics* 9 (2008): 15–26.

Hines, Sandra. "Scientists Ramp Up Ability of Poplar Plants to Disarm Toxic Pollutants," University of Washington Office of News and Infor-mation Web Site. Available online. URL: http://uwnews.washington.edu/ni/article.asp?articleID=37313.

Holden, Matthew T.G., Richard W. Titball, Sharon J. Peacock, Ana M. Cerdeño-Tárraga, Timothy Atkins, Lisa C. Crossman, Tyrone Pitt et al. "Genomic Plasticity of the Causative Agent of Melioidosis, *Burkholderia pseudomallei.*" *Proceedings of the National Academy of Science, USA* 101 (2004): 14240–14245.

Holliday, Robin. "Epigenetics: A Historical Overview." *Epigenetics* 1 (2006): 76–80.

Hu, Wei, Bernd Kieseier, Elliot Frohman, Todd N. Eagar, Roger N. Rosen-berg, Hans-Peter Hartung , and Olaf Stüve. "Prion Proteins: Physiologi-cal Functions and Role in Neurological Disorders." *Journal of the Neuro-logical Sciences* 264 (2008): 1–8.

Hunter, Graeme K. *Vital Forces: The Discovery of the Molecular Basis of Life.* New York: Academic Press, 2000.

Ibrahim, Youssef M. "Genetic Soybeans Alarm Europeans." *The New York Times*, November 7, 1996.

"Insights Learned from the Sequence," Human Genome Project Informa-tion Site. Available online. URL: http://www.ornl.gov/sci/techresources/Human_Genome/project/journals/insights.html.

"Investigation of Human Health Effects Associated with Potential Expo-sure to Genetically Modified Corn," Centers for Disease Control and Prevention Web Site. Available online. URL: http://www.cdc.gov/nceh/ehhe/Cry9cReport/summary.htm.

Jablonka, Eva and Marion J. Lamb. "The Changing Concept of Epigenetics."*Annals of the New York Academy of Sciences* 981 (2002): 82–96.

Johnson, Sarah Stewart, Martin B. Hebsgaard, Torben Christensen, Mikhail Mastepanov, Rasmus Nielsen, Kasper Munch, Tina Brand et al., "An-cient Bacteria Show Evidence of DNA Repair." *Proceedings of the Na-tional Academy of Science, USA* 104 (2007):14401–14405.

Jones, Peter A. and Daiya Takai. "The Role of DNA Methylation in Mammalian Epigenetics." *Science* 293 (2001): 1068–1070.

Kehrer-Sawatzki, Hildegard and David N. Cooper. "Understanding the Recent Evolution of the Human Genome: Insights from Human–Chimpanzee Genome Comparisons." *Human Mutation* 28 (2007): 99–130.

Kim, Daniel H. and John J. Rossi. "Strategies for Silencing Human Disease Using RNA Interference." *Nature Reviews Genetics* 8 (2007): 173–184.

Klug, Aaron. "The Discovery of the DNA Double Helix." *Journal of Molecular Biology* 335 (2004): 3–26.

Kouzarides, Tony. "Chromatin Modifications and Their Function." *Cell* 128 (2007): 693–705.

Leung, Ray K.M. and Paul A. Whittaker. "RNA Interference: From Gene Silencing to Gene-specific Therapeutics." *Pharmacology & Therapeutics* 107 (2005): 222–239.

Levy, Samuel, Granger Sutton, Pauline C. Ng, Lars Feuk, Aaron L. Halpern, Brian P. Walenz, Nelson Axelrod et al. "The Diploid Genome Sequence of an Individual Human." *PLoS Biology* 5 (2007): 2113–2144.

Lin, William, Gregory K. Price, and Edward Allen. "Starlink™: Where No Cry9c Corn Should Have Gone Before." *Choices* 17 (2002): 31–34.

Little, Peter F.R. "Structure and Function of the Human Genome." *Genome Research* 15 (2005): 1759–1766.

Luedi, Philippe P., Fred S. Dietrich, Jennifer R. Weidman, Jason M. Bosko, Randy L. Jirtle, and Alexander J. Hartemink. "Computational and Experimental Identification of Novel Human Imprinted Genes." *Genome Research* 17 (2007): 1723–1730.

Marengo-Rowe, Alain. J. "Structure-function Relations of Human Hemoglobins." *Baylor University Medical Center Proceedings* 19 (2006): 239–245.

Marks, Paul. "Genetically Modified Yeast Can Sniff Out Explosives." *New Scientist* (May 9, 2007): 30.

"The Marshall W. Nirenberg Papers: Public Reactions to the Genetic Code, 1961–1968," National Library of Medicine Web Site. Available online. URL: http://profiles.nlm.nih.gov/JJ/Views/Exhibit/narrative/publicreaction.html.

Matthews, Qiana L. and David T. Curiel. "Gene Therapy: Human Germline Genetic Modifications—Assessing the Scientific, Socioethical, and Religious Issues." *Southern Medical Journal* 100 (2007): 98–100.

Melo, Eduardo O., Aurea M.O. Canavessi, Mauricio M. Franco, and Rodolfo Rumpf. "Animal Transgenesis: State of the Art and Applications." *Journal of Applied Genetics* 48 (2007): 47–61.

Morange, Michel. *A History of Molecular Biology.* Cambridge, Mass.: Harvard University Press, 1998.

Morrow, John F., Stanley N. Cohen, Annie C.Y. Chang, Herbert W. Boyer, Howard M. Goodman, and Robert B. Helling. "Replication and Transcription of Eukaryotic DNA in *Escherichia coli.*" *Proceedings of the National Academy of Science, USA* 71 (1974): 1743–1747.

Muin, J. Khoury, Linda L. McCabe, and Edward R.B. McCabe. "Population Screening in the Age of Genomic Medicine." *The New England Journal of Medicine* 348 (2003): 50–58.

Murray, Robert K., Daryl K. Granner, and Victor W. Rodwell. *Harper's Illustrated Biochemistry,* 27th ed. New York: Lange Medical Books/McGraw-Hill, 2006.

Nanjundiah, Vidyanand. "George Gamow and the Genetic Code." *Resonance* 9 (2004): 44–49.

Niemann, H., W. Kues, and J.W. Carnwath. "Transgenic Farm Animals: Present and Future." *Scientific and Technical Review* 24 (2005): 285–298.

Nierman, William C., David DeShazer, H. Stanley Kim, Herve Tettelin, Karen E. Nelson, Tamara Feldblyum, Ricky L. Ulrich et al. "Structural Flexibility in the *Burkholderia mallei* Genome." *Proceedings of the National Academy of Science, USA* 101 (2004): 14246–14251.

Nirenberg, Marshall W. "Will Society be Prepared?" *Science* 157 (1967): 633.

Nirenberg, Marshall. "Historical Review: Deciphering the Genetic Code— A Personal Account." *Trends in Biochemical Sciences* 29 (2004): 46–54.

Nussbaum, Robert L., Roderick R. McInnes, Huntington F. Willard, and Ada Hamosh. *Thompson & Thompson Genetics in Medicine,* 7th ed. Philadelphia: Saunders Elsevier, 2007.

Osawa, Syozo. *Evolution of the Genetic Code.* New York: Oxford University Press, 1995.

Ostrander, Elaine A. "Genetics and the Shape of Dogs." *American Scientist* 95 (September–October 2007): 406–413.

Palmiter, Richard D., Ralph L. Brinster, Robert E. Hammer, Myrna E. Trumbauer, Michael G. Rosenfeld, Neal C. Birnberg, and Ronald M. Evans. "Dramatic Growth of Mice That Develop from Eggs Microinjected with Metallothionein–growth Hormone Fusion Genes." *Nature* 300 (1982): 611–615.

"Pharmacogenomics and the Future of 'Personalized Medicine'," *Today's Science on File* 13 (2005): 279–281.

"Pharmaco-What? Introducing Personalized Medicine," The University of Utah, Genetic Science Learning Center Web Site. Available online. URL: http://learn.genetics.utah.edu/units/pharma/phwhatis/.

Schwartz, Mark I. "Fear versus Science." *International Herald Tribune*, December 14, 2007. Available online. URL: http://www.iht.com.

Singh, Om V., Shivani Ghai, Debarati Paul, and Rakesh K. Jain. "Genetically Modified Crops: Success, Safety Assessment, and Public Concern." *Applied Microbiology and Biotechnology* 71 (2006): 598–607.

Reik, Wolf. "Stability and Flexibility of Epigenetic Gene Regulation in Mammalian Development." *Nature* 447 (2007): 425–432.

Rodenhiser, David and Mellissa Mann. "Epigenetics and Human Disease: Translating Basic Biology into Clinical Applications." *Canadian Medical Association Journal* 174 (2006): 341–348.

Santos, Fátima and Wendy Dean. "Epigenetic Reprogramming During Early Development in Mammals." *Reproduction* 127 (2004): 643–651.

"A Science Primer," National Center for Biotechnology Information Web Site. Available online. URL: http://www.ncbi.nlm.nih.gov/About/primer/genetics_cell.html.

Sharrer, G. Terry. "The Great Glanders Epizootic, 1861–1866: A Civil War Legacy." *Agricultural History* 69 (1995): 79–97.

Singh, Simon. *The Code Book*. New York: Anchor Books, 1999.

Spök, Armin. "Molecular Farming on the Rise—GMO Regulators Still Walking a Tightrope." *Trends in Biotechnology* 25 (2007): 74–82.

Stewart, C. Neal. "Go with the Glow: Fluorescent Proteins to Light Transgenic Organisms." *Trends in Biotechnology* 24 (2006): 155–162.

Stone, Anne C., James E. Starrs, and Mark Stoneking. "Mitochondrial DNA Analysis of the Presumptive Remains of Jesse James." *Journal of Forensic Science* 46 (2001): 173–176.

Strachan, Tom and Andrew Read. *Human Molecular Genetics,* 3rd ed. London: Garland Science Publishing, 2003.

Sutter, Nathan B., Carlos D. Bustamante, Kevin Chase, Melissa M. Gray, Keyan Zhao, Lan Zhu, Badri Padhukasahasram et al. "A Single IGF1 Allele Is a Major Determinant of Small Size in Dogs." *Science* 316 (2007): 112–115.

Thayer, Ann. "Insulin." *Chemical & Engineering News* 83 (2005): 74–75.

Thompson, Larry. "Are Bioengineered Foods Safe?" *FDA Consumer Magazine* 34 (January–February 2000). Available online. URL: http://www.fda.gov/fdac/fdacindex.html.

Thompson, Larry. "Human Gene Therapy: Harsh Lessons, High Hopes." *FDA Consumer Magazine* 34 (September–October 2000). Available online. URL: http://www.fda.gov/fdac/fdacindex.html.

Travis, Emma R., Nerissa K. Hannink, Christopher J. van der Gast, Ian P. Thompson, Susan J. Rosser, and Neil C. Bruce. "Impact of Transgenic Tobacco on Trinitrotoluene (TNT) Contaminated Soil Community." *Environmental Science & Technology* 41 (2007): 5854–5861.

Ubell, Earl. "The Code of Life Finally Cracked." *New York Herald Tribune*, December 24, 1961.

Vajo, Zoltan, Janet Fawcett, and William C. Duckworth. "Recombinant DNA Technology in the Treatment of Diabetes: Insulin Analogs." *Endocrine Reviews* 22 (2001): 706–717.

Van Boven, H.H., R.J. Olds, S.-L. Thein, P.H. Reitsma, D.A. Lane, E. Briët, J.P. Vandenbroucke et al. "Hereditary Antithrombin Deficiency: Heterogeneity of the Molecular Basis and Mortality in Dutch Families." *Blood* 84 (1994): 4209–4213.

Van Vliet, J., N.A. Oates, and E. Whitelaw. "Epigenetic Mechanisms in the Context of Complex Diseases." *Cellular and Molecular Life Sciences* 64 (2007): 1531–1538.

Varki, Ajit and Tasha K. Altheide. "Comparing the Human and Chimpanzee Genomes: Searching for Needles in a Haystack." *Genome Research* 15 (2005): 1746–1758.

Verma, Inder M. and Matthew D. Weitzman. "Gene Therapy: Twenty-First Century Medicine." *Annual Reviews of Biochemistry* 74 (2005): 711–738.

Vinci, Victor A. and Sarad R. Parekh, eds. *Handbook of Industrial Cell Culture: Mammalian, Microbial, and Plant Cells.* Totowa, New Jersey: Humana Press, 2002.

Walsh, Gary. *Biopharmaceuticals: Biochemistry and Biotechnology.* New York: John Wiley & Sons, 1998.

Watson, J.D. and F.H.C. Crick. "A Structure for Deoxyribose Nucleic Acid." *Nature* 171 (1953): 737–738.

Watson, James D., Amy A. Caudy, Richard M. Myers, and Jan A. Witkowski. *Recombinant DNA: Genes and Genomes — A Short Course,* 3rd ed. New York: W.H. Freeman and Company, 2007.

Weber, Michael and Dirk Schübeler. "Genomic Patterns of DNA Methylation: Targets and Function of an Epigenetic Mark." *Current Opinion in Cell Biology* 19 (2007): 273–280.

Weidman, Jennifer R., Dana C. Dolinoy, Susan K. Murphy, and Randy L. Jirtle. "Cancer Susceptibility: Epigenetic Manifestation of Environmental Exposures." *The Cancer Journal* 13 (2007): 9–16.

"What are Genetic Disorders?" The University of Utah, Genetic Science Learning Center Web Site. Available online. URL: http://learn.genetics. utah.edu/units/disorders/whataregd/.

Woo, Savio L.C. "Researchers React to Gene Therapy's Pitfalls and Promises." *FDA Consumer Magazine* 34 (September–October 2000). Available online. URL: http://www.fda.gov/fdac/fdacindex.html.

Wrixon, Fred B. *Codes, Ciphers, Secrets and Cryptic Communication.* New York: Black Dog & Leventhal, 1998.

Zeviani, Massimo and Valerio Carelli. "Mitochondrial Disorders." *Current Opinion in Neurology* 20 (2007): 564–571.

Further Resources

Bankston, John. *Francis Crick and James Watson: Pioneers in DNA Research*. Hockessin, Delaware: Mitchell Lane Publishers, 2002.

Claybourne, Anna. *Introduction to Genes and DNA*. London: Usborne Publishing Limited, 2003.

Farndon, John. *From DNA to GM Wheat: Discovering Genetically Modified Food*. Chicago: Heinemann, 2007.

Fridell, Ron. *Decoding Life: Unraveling the Mysteries of the Genome*. Minneapolis: Lerner Publishing Group, 2004.

Hopkins, William G. *Plant Biotechnology*. New York: Chelsea House Publishers, 2006.

Morris, Jonathan. *The Ethics of Biotechnology*. New York: Chelsea House Publishers, 2005.

Panno, Joseph. *Gene Therapy*. New York: Chelsea House Publishers, 2004.

Phelan, Glen. *Double Helix*. Washington, D.C.: National Geographic Children's Books, 2006.

Schacter, Bernice. *Biotechnology and Your Health*. New York: Chelsea House Publishers, 2005.

Snedden, Robert. *DNA and Genetic Engineering*. Chicago: Heinemann, 2002.

Walker, Richard. *Genes and DNA*. New York: Houghton Mifflin Company, 2003.

Web Sites

Biotech Applied
http://www.accessexcellence.org/RC/AB/BA/

The National Health Museum describes the many ways that scientists have applied biotechnology in the areas of medicine, agriculture, and forensics.

Deciphering the Genetic Code
http://history.nih.gov/exhibits/nirenberg/index.htm

> *Sponsored by the National Institutes of Health, this Web site shows how scientists cracked the genetic code. The site also provides information on scientific instruments used to understand the code.*

GeneTests
http://www.ncbi.nlm.nih.gov/sites/GeneTests/?db=GeneTests

> *This Web site offers information about genetic testing and an illustrated glossary of terms.*

Genetic Science Learning Center
http://learn.genetics.utah.edu/

> *The University of Utah provides a wide range of information about genetics. Here, readers can tour colorful presentations on basic functions of DNA, RNA, and proteins, before reviewing advanced topics, such as gene therapy, transgenic mice, and epigenetics.*

Genomics and Its Impact on Science and Society
http://www.ornl.gov/sci/techresources/Human_Genome/publicat/primer2001/index.shtml

> *The Human Genome Program offers information on new methods of genetic analysis and insights into societal concerns raised by the use of these techniques.*

Online Mendelian Inheritance in Man
http://www.ncbi.nlm.nih.gov/sites/entrez?db=omim

> *The Online Mendelian Inheritance in Man Web site provides information about all known genetic diseases in humans.*

A Revolution in Progress: Human Genetics and Medical Research
http://history.nih.gov/exhibits/genetics/index.htm

> *Here, readers will find information about diagnosing and treating genetic disorders, as well as ethical questions raised by genetic testing.*

YourGenome.org
http://www.yourgenome.org/

> *This Web site offers insights into basic genetics and genetic engineering. Readers will also learn how drug therapy may be tailored to a person's genome.*

Picture Credits

Index

About the Author

Phill Jones earned a Ph.D. in Physiology/Pharmacology from the University of California, San Diego. After completing postdoctoral training at Stanford University School of Medicine, he joined the Department of Biochemistry at the University of Kentucky Medical Center as an assistant professor. Here, he taught topics in molecular biology and medicine and researched aspects of gene expression. He later earned a JD at the University of Kentucky College of Law and worked ten years as a patent attorney, specializing in biological, chemical, and medical inventions. Dr. Jones is now a full-time writer. His articles have appeared in *Today's Science on File*, *The World Almanac and Book of Facts*, *History Magazine*, *Forensic Magazine*, *Genomics and Proteomics Magazine*, *Encyclopedia of Forensic Science*, *The Science of Michael Crichton*, *Forensic Nurse Magazine*, *Nature Biotechnology*, *Information Systems for Biotechnology News Report*, *Law and Order Magazine*, *PharmaTechnology Magazine*, and publications for use by the Florida Department of Education. He also wrote and teaches an online course in forensic science for writers.

Phill Jones dedicates his book:
"To my parents, who encouraged my fascination with science."